'... A country residence, lig
slight repair. Inside it was c
had fallen in and the wind sur͜ ....ough the rafters. A
ladder led up to the planking upon which lay broken
tiles, mixed with pigeon excrement ...'

'... And only six hundred thousand francs ...'

So began the search of the author and his wife for a
second home in France. Yet from such inauspicious
beginnings the Pilkingtons succeeded in becoming part
of a very natural and charming vine-growing community. In a land where they were both strangers.

Sharply observed and written in an easy style by an
expert on France, this book is a mine of information for
Francophiles who want to settle (or dream of it) in
France as well as being a good read full of humorous
anecdotes.

☆　☆　☆

Originally a research geneticist at Cambridge, Roger
Pilkington gradually moved over to writing. He has
had more than fifty books published including twenty
in the popular *Small Boat . . .* series which established
the idea of inland cruising on continental waterways.

These voyages gave birth to a series of children's
adventure books, one of which was on the BBC's
Jackanory programme. The author has made regular
contributions, often on walking, to *The Sunday Telegraph*.
He and his wife divide their time between Jersey and
their house in Montouliers in France, where they
produce wine from two small vineyards.

Other books by Roger Pilkington include:

Twenty volumes of the '*Small Boat . . .*' series, from *Small Boat through Belgium* (1957) to *Small Boat in the Midi* (1989), Children's adventures, from *Jan's Treasure* (1955) to *The Ormering Tide* (1974) and *I Sailed on the Mayflower* (1990)

Scientific or Religious works, including:

In The Beginning
World without End
Heavens Alive
Revelation through Science
Robert Boyle – Father of Chemistry
The Ways of the Sea
Sons and Daughters

ONE FOOT IN FRANCE

Roger Pilkington

Temple House Books
Sussex, England

Illustrations by Agneta Stålhand

Temple House Books
is an imprint of
The Book Guild Ltd.

The Book Guild Ltd.
25 High Street,
Lewes, Sussex

Hard back edition first published 1992
© Roger Pilkington 1992

Paper edition published 1993

Set in Baskerville

Typesetting by Raven Typesetters
Ellesmere Port, South Wirral

Printed in Great Britain by
Antony Rowe Ltd.
Chippenham, Wiltshire.

A catalogue record for this book is
available from the British Library

ISBN 0 86332 936 5

CONTENTS

Foreword

After more than thirty years in which every holiday bar one
had been spent on the canals and rivers of Europe, I had
reluctantly come to realise that in future my feet should
prudently be on solid ground. Falling off lock-gates on to a steel
boat below may be comic stuff to the spectator but is less
amusing to the faller, and although it was now ten years since I
had done so when descending the River Doubs to Besançon, I
still remembered it as an experience best not repeated. Besides,
at seventy years of age the increased brittleness of the bones
could be a complicating factor.

And even more, there was Ingrid, my wife, to be considered.
Over the years she had become an incomparable expert at
stepping from a moving boat to the slimy and weed-hung
ladder on the outside of a lock-gate, the nooses of two heavy
lines over her shoulder so that she could climb rapidly up, drop
the ropes smartly over two bollards forty yards apart and then
run to crank the gate shut while I stopped the craft, hauled the
lines tight fore and aft, and repelled any holiday boatmen who
jabbed at everything within range with their pointed harpoons
of boat-hooks. Our teamwork was perfect. We were a pair of
expert lockers if ever there was one, and we had once achieved
thirty-nine locks in a single day, unaided. But again, at the age
of seventy, one could conceivably miss a footing and be left
hanging upside down on the lock-gate.

Ingrid agreed that the time had come to think ahead, to
consider dry land as an alternative, to find a place to put the
pied on French *terre*, she said.

But why French? After all, we both spoke German fluently
from our student days in the thirties, so why choose France?

We discussed the matter in what civil servants call 'depth',
and had no difficulty in deciding that we could rule out
Germany and all lands to the north or west because of their

weather, which ranged from unreasonable to atrocious. We could reject Switzerland because it seemed to us artificial, Greece because it was too far away from Jersey, Spain and Italy because we felt that the tourist industry was gradually robbing them of their essential character. It had to be France. Besides, that was the country we knew, and loved.

Yes, France it must be. We knew the country from north to south, and from east to west. We had canalled it several times on our way from London or Stockholm to the Mediterranean, and we knew many areas of great charm familiar to bargees but never visited by the English or the Swedes. I myself had walked throughout Provence and in the Natural Park containing more than ninety extinct volcanoes which was situated in the Massif Central. We had seen from harbours the whole of the Côte d'Azur – and had left it as rapidly as possible. But we had also been in many parts of the Languedoc, and it was this part of France, where they once used to speak a tongue or *langue* in which one said '*Oc*' instead of '*Oui*', which drew us like a magnet. None could rival it for sheer beauty, and an absence of the hurry and flurry of Paris and the North.

Cartographically the Languedoc encompassed the whole of the country south of the Loire and west of the Rhone, and that was a vast area. Clearly we had to reduce the field of choice in some way. Our first help came unexpectedly when we were staying with friends in Mazamet and drove one day south-eastward, climbing up through the dripping woodlands and past sodden meadows grazed by mournful sheep to emerge unexpectedly from the forest south of St. Pons-de-Thomières into a totally different landscape. It was a countryside bathed in brilliant light, a land dry and rosemary-scented, with wide views stretching over rugged country toward the distant sea which could just be seen, or at least imagined, as a line of silver on the horizon. It was as though we were in another land, with another climate.

In fact we were. The divide between the Atlantic and Mediterranean climates lay along the ridge of those hills south of St. Pons. In winter – as we were soon to discover – it could be snowing on the northern side but warm and dry on the southern slopes, and the transition from the one environment to the other was completely accomplished within only a few hundred metres near the hamlet of St. Colombe. The tall,

8

sombre beeches gave way to a scrub of prickly evergreen oaks, the cowslips to the pink, orange-centred cystus, the flocks of sheep to patches of geometrically precise rows of vines wherever there was soil enough for their roots.

That area south of the divide was the Minervois, and its hills rolled away southward to the plain of the Aude, beyond which were the wild and sun-baked tracts of the Corbières. In one or other of those areas we would find our second home, we were sure. And from that day's decision we never looked back.

Roger Pilkington
Montouliers, 1992

1

The First Foothold

The Minervois was not entirely new to us. We had crossed it at least a dozen times by boat, following the curiously meandering course of the Canal du Midi where it curved around the contours of the last expiring slopes of the Cevennes. It was easy enough to decide that no area could suit us better as a possible tract in which to place our feet, but actually to find a suitable location was another matter. The countryside was not very heavily populated, and we knew from our explorations over the years by boat or on land that there were many attractive, peaceful villages. However we could see no evidence of anything for sale in the area other than deserted ruins. Of course we knew that there were agencies in London which had lists of French properties for sale, but we reckoned that if a house had to be advertised abroad this could only mean that it was unsaleable in the country itself, or that ridiculous prices were being asked on the assumption that the English were stupid, or careless about money, or millionaires, or all three at once. It seemed more sensible, therefore, to try a local approach, so on the advice of French friends in a neighbouring *département* we sought out an agency in Carcassonne, the county town of the Aude, and sent details describing precisely the kind of property we had in mind. A rendezvous was agreed for the second day of January, as we thought it would be wise to see any properties when the likelihood of rain, snow and gales was at its highest.

Actually, the day proved fine enough, though with a biting wind – the Tramontane that we were soon to know so well. We drove with our friends following behind the agent, who was accompanied by her mother who wanted an afternoon drive. We wound to and fro along minor roads to the south of the Canal du Midi until the lady stopped at a kink in a country lane just outside a hamlet which overlooked the valley of the Aude.

'I am convinced that you will adore this one,' the Carcassonne house-agent said. 'It is impeccable, it is not? A real country property, and you can assure yourself that the situation is unique. And the view! Why, down there one can make out the course of the Canal du Midi.'

She adjusted her hair, which was being tugged by the cold and savage blast of the Tramontane sweeping off the snowy mountains hidden away in the distant north.

'Yes, it is a dream,' she continued. 'And the proprietor is a man very serious, very serious indeed. He would never be willing to sell except to oblige very exceptional people. But for you, I am sure, he would make the real sacrifice,' she purred. '*Mais oui!* I am sure we need look no further.'

We stepped politely across a bed of nettles and a layer of dried cow manure to the building, described on the mimeographed sheet from her files as a country residence, light and airy, yet in need of slight repair. It was a long barn for wains, devoid of any windows but with the rotted remains of a high double door through which once the carts had passed. Inside it was certainly light and airy, for the roof had fallen in and the wind surged through the rafters. A ladder led up to the planking upon which lay broken tiles, mixed with pigeon excrement.

'And only six hundred thousand francs . . .'

'Old ones, of course?' One could never be sure. It was now a quarter of a century since the franc had been devalued by a factor of one hundred, but some people habitually thought and talked in terms of the older currency – just as I myself always transmuted 'p' or new pence into 's.&d.' in order to be sure of the value of a thing.

'*Non, non. Non, non, non.* Not centimes. Six hundred thousand francs, *bien sur.*' She nodded sagely, and wrote the figure on a piece of paper to make certain that these block-headed customers could understand it.

'Ah.'

The agent looked at us winningly. 'You think it is expensive? The owner is a good man, very correct. He would never demand a price beyond what is reasonable. How much would you offer for it?'

'Nothing.'

We drove on, and our next call was at a deserted piggery in the now dry marsh of Marseillette where the styes, we were told, could without unreasonable expense be made higher to form a residence *très chic.* Just the thing for upper crust porkers, I thought. We then were taken to view half a house at Conques-sur-Orbiel, with the main road traffic brushing the withered leaves off the geraniums which were hibernating in sawn-off detergent drums on the window-sills.

'No? It does not please you? *Vraiment?*'

'*Vraiment.*'

She clicked her tongue, shrugged, then decided to try an encouraging smile. These English were often difficult, she knew from experience. They were not like the Dutch, who would jump at the opportunity of buying any ruin that was on the market, provided it was cheap. But the English . . .

'I have kept the best until last,' she said boldly. 'You are a lover of the canals, yes? And this house is right beside the Canal du Midi! Come, we shall hurry to Le Somail while there is still daylight.'

I knew Le Somail well. It was a hamlet grouped around a particularly pretty and very hump-backed bridge flanked by a chapel, and a restaurant where I once had the second worst meal I was ever served in France. (The worst, as well as the best was in the Cité de Carcassonne.) The prospect was not unattractive, I thought, for when retired from boating one could perhaps sit on a bollard and emulate Coleridge's ancient mariner, grabbing hold of every third person in a wedding party and boring them with highly improbable tales. Yes, Le Somail had its points. Or so we thought, until we saw the house, a nondescript mess of a place in a nondescript and messy row of dwellings in a run-down road which was not even within sight of the canal.

We thanked the agent for taking so much trouble. No, we did not wish further properties to look at. If we needed madame's exceptional knowledge and advice again we would telephone her.

Next day we explored on our own, and in the late morning we came to Argeliers, a village we knew well from years of voyages. It was brushed by a meandering loop of the canal, where the long level followed the contour of the foot of the hills. It was nearing the hour of the French lunchtime when we arrived there, and any stores there might be were already closing, except for the bakery and the *charcuterie*, where an attractive and smiling *charcutière* was sweeping the sawdust into a corner.

Was there an *agence immobilière* in the place? *Bien sur!* That is, Monsieur and Madame le Grix had an agency in Narbonne, but they drove back every day for lunch. They lived there, just opposite. Our informant pointed at a wedge-shaped building which looked like a primitive garage and had a solid wooden door closed with a padlock. There appeared to be no windows, at least none on the ground floor.

The *charcutière* looked at her watch. Five to twelve. 'Soon they will close their office in Narbonne, then they will drive back here. Then of course there will be the lunch . . . one hour, perhaps one and a half. You come back after two o'clock?'

This was our first introduction to the holy hour, the customary three-hour lunch break of the ordinary Frenchman, or at least of the Languedocian. I could hardly imagine anyone in England driving twenty miles to work, driving home again at midday, driving back again to reach the office after three, and then home once more at tea-time – not for tea, of course, because the French stomach has left no room for more fluid after consuming a bottle of wine with the lunch, but tea-time in the English sense, time to shut up shop. And all that, regardless of expense, in order to be able to sit down to an *apéritif*, then a second *apéritif*, a whale of a lunch with *vin rouge*, a tiny cup of coffee and a *digestif* to sustain the gastric juices during another couple of hours in the office. Over the months ahead I discovered that the most dangerous time of day on the French roads was between half past two and half past three, when drivers of everything from Deux Chevaux to Mercedes might be somnolent, unsteady, myopic, heroic, and worried about being late back at the office.

When we returned to Argeliers the hasp had been unlocked on the dry and decaying double door to reveal an inner door of small glass panes. We knocked, and a short and somewhat obese man with a Parisian moustache rose, wiped his mouth, and invited us in a cloud of garlic to enter. A smiling, roundish woman with a fur coat down to her ankles was cooking something at the stove. A younger man with a lesser moustache was lighting a cigarette. Monsieur and Madame Robert le Grix and their son Bruno were just concluding their meal.

The air was thick with wood-smoke, fumes, the smell of roasting, and *caporal*. It was just the right time to intrude and join the family in a glass of Minervois rouge from the nearby co-operative. The wine was warming, and the great fire of logs at the end of the table soon had us pleasantly tingling.

We were looking for a house? *Mais oui*, of course there were houses for sale, right here in the village. After lunch Bruno would show them to us.

And so he did. Bruno was somewhat off-hand and un-communicative, leaning against the wall and smoking another cigarette while we studied the aspect of one or two village houses tucked away in the alleys behind the *Mairie*. He took us to see a new standard bungalow which an ever-expanding family now found too small for their needs. It was prosaic, a mean little house with a tiny attempt at a flower-bed along the side facing the road. All the houses on offer were infinitely better than those of the madame at Carcassonne, but we could not imagine ourselves settling happily in any one of them. We said as much to Bruno.

He shrugged. He clearly had no high opinion of these fusspots who wanted sanitation, a view over the countryside, and even such a ridiculous object as a bath.

'*C'est tout*,' he declared without much enthusiasm. 'Except that there is a house in the Dutch village.'

15

'The Dutch village?'

'*Oui. Le village Hollandais.*' He lit another cigarette.

'And where is that?'

'Not far. Ten minutes.' He was bored with us, but we said we would go with him and see this Dutch village and the house.

In later years nothing would have persuaded us to buy a property in 'Soleil d'Oc', the *village Hollandais* a few kilometres beyond Pouzols and to the side of the main road from Béziers to Carcassonne, but that little house gave us our first spare home on firm ground in the Languedoc, and the chance to explore one of the loveliest areas of France, and indeed of all Europe.

Some of the houses were garage-sized boxes near the main road, but at the top there were indeed three with a reasonable amount of land all around them, and an unobstructed outlook over a rough heathland towards woods and hillocks which stretched away beyond the vineyards to the valley of the Aude and the coastal headland massif of La Clape in the far distance. The owner of one of these holiday homes had been killed when flying his small plane, and the house was for sale, just as it stood and with everything that was in it, right down to the paperbacks in Dutch. We liked the place, were sure we could improve it to meet our own wishes, and on the following day we signed the contract in le Grix's Narbonne office.

We were now introduced to the French system. To buy or sell a property is not just a matter of signing a contract, handing over money, and seeing that the title is transferred and duly registered. Two notaries are needed, and details of the proposed transfer are stated on a form which has to leap, or rather crawl, over three successive hurdles of *préemption*. The property has first to be offered to the State, and we could imagine M. Mitterand looking up from dipping his croissant in his coffee, giving his peculiar twisted smile, and declining the offer with a wave of his hand. Next, it is offered to the *département*, which might wish to put a swimming-pool, or a spur for the motorway, or a home for retired civil servants there. Finally, it goes to the *commune*, and it is the stamp of the local *Mairie* which finally clears the way for the transaction to go ahead. But these official events do not follow each other at once. There are delays, the papers being stalled each time in the office of the vendor's lawyer, who is generally suspected of delaying things for his own advantage, so that he can put the money on deposit and keep the interest himself. French friends who should know – and who incidentally are not themselves notaries – assure me that this is not the case, and that even if the lawyer's fees for procuring the transfer may amount to as much as 13% of the purchase price, this is (they say) because much of the charge has to be disbursed to various official bodies in taxes and the like, the lawyer himself managing to exist (albeit very often in a splendid period mansion) on a mere pittance of the sum paid over by the one who is buying the property.

Le Grix told us that these formalities would take about twelve weeks, maybe more. I said we would not accept any 'maybe-mores'. He replied that we might have to. It was normal that twelve weeks would suffice, but who could say? However, the contract would take care of that. *Courage!* The paper would be drawn up at once, we would sign it, and then . . .

'And then? Just wait?'

'*Oui, oui. Oh, la la!* France was a land of papers was it not?'

I never was one to ignore the small print on the back of agreements of any kind, so I borrowed a lens and scanned the microscopic, pale grey paragraphs. Then Ingrid and I both had to write: '*Lu et approuvé. Bon pour achat*' in our own handwriting. We were given one copy of the contract and soon we were on our way home once more to Jersey. And to wait.

We had to have a lawyer of course, and we happened to know one in Capestang. The Dutch lady and her mother employed a *notaire* in Montpellier. Weeks passed, during which we had occasional talks over the phone with the widow in Holland. Another month passed. Our lawyer could get no information from his counterpart in the Minervois but he doubted that M. Mitterand, or the Prefect of the Aude, or even the mayor of Pouzols were particularly interested in cutting us out. More weeks passed, and the owner had no news from her notary either. We still waited.

Then, just before four o'clock one morning early in April, I awoke with an idea. Could I be right? Was there not something in that faint print that I had *lu et approuvé*? I jumped out of bed, ran downstairs and with shaking hands opened my filing cabinet, found the copy of the contract and smoothed it out on my desk. I had a magnifying glass at hand, and . . . Yes! There is was! *Lu et approuvé* by Mevrouw the lady in Holland herself.

I rushed upstairs and woke Ingrid, who was very reasonably alarmed to find me waving a piece of paper and shouting 'Eureka!' I thought it decent to wait until seven o'clock Dutch time before ringing Mevrouw, and then I asked her gently if she had read the small print. No, she had not, so far as she could remember.

'I think I ought to read it to you,' I said. And I did, slowly and clearly. The contract stated that if the vendor did not complete the sale and give vacant possession of the premises by noon (the beginning of the holy lunch hour for notaries, as for others) on the day three calendar months from the date of signature of the contract, there was a penalty of thirty-five thousand francs, the contract was void, and all the legal costs of both sides of the transaction were payable by the vendor. Then, as courteously as possible, I mentioned that there were only two days and five hours to go. She should phone her notary at once, I suggested.

In a somewhat shaky voice she thanked me for the warning. She doubtless phoned her lawyer as soon as his office opened, but she was taking no chances. That same morning she and her mother were on the express to Paris, and the following morning on the doorstep of the notary. With the completion duly signed she phoned us in Jersey to thank us once more and to tell us that Number Twenty Soleil d'Oc was really and truly, completely and legally ours. She wished us every happiness there.

That happiness was not long delayed. We gave away the Dutch furniture to people in the village of Pouzols, and began to bring the little house up to a high standard of comfort and convenience with insulation, and a modern kitchen. We also moved a few door openings to change the situation of the loo from Dutch style (opening straight out of the living room, with an unabashed view of the plumbing) to English/Swedish fashion with greater reticence and less in the way of sound effects. In all this we had the excellent services of Jan Griffioen.

Jan was, of course, Dutch. As a conscientious objector (a fact which immediately endeared him to me) he had been obliged to take service overseas instead of in the military. He had been sent out to the Ivory Coast as a labourer to work in some sort of relief project. In this way he had come to learn the building trade, and by a curious stroke of luck he had worked in a Franco-phone land where building was conducted in Anglophone, and thus it came about that when he returned to Europe he knew all about building – in three languages.

For us this was ideal. We could discuss all the details in English and in sensible units of feet and inches, and then Jan could deal with suppliers of materials and his own workmen in French and in metric units. He had arrived in the Languedoc with a single suitcase, he had married a local girl (Martine, whom we came to know well) and was soon established in business as a builder, and a very competent one. Naturally he had all the trade of the Soleil d'Occers, for when the Dutch came back to their houses in the summer months they usually found all kinds of depredations due to damp, or frost, or rodents.

That summer we moved in, or at least partly in. We would come up at lunchtime and cook on a small Camping Gaz stove set on the rough flagstones in front of the verandah, because we had no kitchen. Jan and his men were taking the inside of the house to pieces, and we did not wish to disturb them by being always present during working hours. So we continued to live aboard the *Thames Commodore* at the canal junction only a few kilometres distant, which gave us the opportunity not only to view progress every evening but to explore the neighbourhood too.

The approach to Soleil d'Oc was anything but encouraging. The main road to Carcassonne from Béziers, a real rocket route at the height of the summer season, ran right past the estate on an embankment, and some of those unfortunate Dutchmen who thought they were buying a view of the sea found that their outlook was more likely to be that of the undersides of lorries and caravans. However, the land rose steeply to the south from the foot of the embankment and the few houses placed over the top of the ridge were out of sight of the traffic altogether. Fortunately, such a one was Number Twenty. Only the kitchen window looked out northward, and even then the road was not only out of sight but distant enough to be hardly audible. But the real delight was the outlook on the other side, where we had the verandah on to which both the living-room and the main bedroom opened out. It was soon to become a wonderful situation for breakfast in dressing-gowns, with the early sun flooding the small hills to the east, and shining in autumn upon the distant vines to give a patchwork of yellows and greens and reds. Closer to hand the *garrigue* was blue with rosemary and lavender, and big clumps of Spanish broom sent their perfume drifting into the house.

Straight ahead, across a *vallon* so steep and bramble-filled as to be impassable, the pinewood spread up to the summit of a higher ridge, beyond which lay the valley threaded by the River Aude and the Canal du Midi, with the little wine village of Roubia – once the domain of a Roman landowner named Robianus – nestling beside the waterway. This woodland had the pleasant name of the Pas de Renard, and more than once we saw foxes in the area.

Northward, beyond the offending main road, was Mont Ségonne, the highest point of the Serre d'Oupia and over nine hundred and fifty feet high. (Opianus, another Roman, was apparently the father of Robianus.) This was an excellent area for walks, the long-distance path GR 77 following its crest for part of its course from Minerve and Mailhac to the Pas de Renard and eventually to the sea near the Spanish border. The Serre d'Oupia always promised surprises. It was a good area for snakes, and the only place where I have ever seen Europe's largest owl, *Bubo bubo* the Eagle owl. The French respectfully call it the Grand Duc, which I think is more flatteringly dignified and appropriate than the rather childish if onomato-poeic christening given to it by Carl von Linné.

At the edge of the Serre d'Oupia was Pouzols village, cramped tightly on a mound and more easy to drive into than out of. Its co-operative produced excellent wines and often won prize medals at Mâcon and elsewhere, but the real claim to fame of the village was probably quite unknown to the villagers themselves, for the pleasantly faded manor house standing among the umbrella pines near the church was once the home of the de la Gardie family, one of whom left home in the sixteenth century as a soldier of fortune and founded a distinguished line in Sweden. Probably the family quickly forgot Pouzols. Court life in the far north as royal chancellor was a much better proposition, provided one had sufficient fur coats. Besides, Queen Christina was fluent in French, as many an educated continental was at that time.

Immediately to our left was a sizeable vineyard kept by an old couple who lived in Narbonne. It sheltered a few rabbits which might nibble our plants, but it kept the Dutch at bay and saved us from having neighbours closer than we wished. To the right, hidden by the thick windbreak of cypresses, were our nearest neighbours, the de Kaases and the van der Borns, each of whom spent little more than one month in the year in their Languedocian homes. We had not yet met them, and our first encounter was of an unexpected nature.

2

Soleil d'Oc Days

It was our habit every summer to take a walk of a few days' duration with one or more members of our family. In years past Ingrid and I had followed trails in the Swedish mountains and in Germany, but now, of course, our interest was in France. I was still able to do walks of a week or so, at six hours or more per day, but Ingrid had retired from these extended rambles. Nevertheless, we usually managed a walk locally on almost every day of the year unless there was one of those rare thunderstorms which were not encouraging to the walker.

This particular year I had selected the Luberon area, a dry and steep but beautiful hill range east of Marseilles and Aix. I knew that if we took one of the paths which crossed it we could be sure of eventually arriving every day at some sort of a settlement where we could secure modest accommodation, adequate if simple plumbing, and a superb evening meal with a bottle of *Côtes du Luberon* rouge. On this occasion I was accompanied by our son Johan, and we started near Sault, passed by St. Saturnin d'Apt, and thence by Roussillon and Gordes to Oppède le Vieux. It was there that I twisted a knee, and although we managed to cross the Luberon to Mérindol, we thought it wise to take the bus out and go back to Soleil d'Oc a day earlier than we had intended.

When we arrived home we expected Ingrid to be surprised. And she was. But her astonishment was nothing compared with mine, for the scene in front of me as we came round the corner of the house was one of utter destruction, a real abomination of desolation – and some of it still smouldering. The house was still there, but the forty small cypresses planted as a hedge and windbreak between ourselves and the de Kaases were now reduced to a row of black stalks, and of the cystuses and lavenders I had planted liberally over our section of the *garrigue* only a few charred remnants remained to show where they had been. Even the grass and a patch of nettles had vanished. Everything other than the house had clearly and literally gone up in smoke.

Ingrid told the story. She had been on her way back from shopping in Olonzac when she noticed a column of black smoke ominously tinged with red rising skywards at the back of the ridge. She raced home to find that Mr van der Born, who like most Dutchmen was an indefatigable gardener, had raked together a lot of dry rubbish, clippings, dead leaves from under the bushes, and other detritus from the past winter, had piled it up in the corner of his garden on the de Kaase side, and had set it alight. The day was not windless, and a sudden gust of Tramontane did the rest for him. Within minutes the flames were racing across the dry land of inflammable shrubs and bushes at astonishing speed. By the time Ingrid arrived back at the house the fire was sweeping past, devouring everything in its path until it reached the neighbouring vineyard, where that part of the conflagration stopped. The *pompiers* from Bize had quickly answered a call and had managed to soak the area ahead of the flames so that the rest of the conflagration had also been stopped before it could run onto the houses at the further end. Only the landscapes of the de Kaases (who were not in residence yet) and the Pilkingtons resembled the ash-heaps that they were.

Ingrid told me that Mrs van der Born had come to call upon her in a state of great agitation. She had been in tears. Her husband had not done it on purpose, really he hadn't. It was the wind that took him by surprise. He was still in a state of collapse, but he would wish me to call round as soon as I came home.

I crossed the scorched earth of our own land and the de Kaases and found Mr van der Born obviously very shaken. Clearly, the most important thing was to calm him down and let his blood pressure return to nearer normal. Nothing was to be gained by telling him how foolish he had been, as he was well aware of the fact and it would not restore our land to the gay and flowery condition of high summer. His wife made me a cup of coffee and we all three sat outside their house amid the scent of his flourishing lavender bushes, the full extent of the destruction mercifully hidden by a bank of broom. Not a hair of the head of a single van der Born plant had even been singed, but wisps of smoke could still be seen rising beyond the broom bushes from the remnants of the de Kaases and Pilkington domaines. Fortunately, neither of the houses had come to any harm at all, because Jan and his men had been on the spot and had promptly sprayed the side of each building with water.

I had not so much as seen van der Born until now, but I liked him. He was a retired schoolmaster from somewhere near Groningen. Under normal circumstances he would have been rather neat and dapper, even if at this first meeting he was very naturally distraught and straggly. He certainly expected me to drop a heavy load of sound and fury upon him, but no amount of raging at him for being such a fool as to light a big bonfire on a windy day was going to bring the shrubs and cypresses back. I assured him that anyone might have done the same (which was hardly true) and that he could forget it, because the insurance would certainly cover it – which inwardly I rather doubted, though in fact they stumped up without demur and we were able to get the nurserymen of La Meyrale to plant the area for the second time in three months.

Gradually, Jan the schoolmaster became calmer, and we turned to talking about the footpaths in the area. It transpired that he was a great walker and explorer of everything from rabbit tracks to *sentiers de grande randonnée*. So at least we had something to occupy our minds instead of endless recriminations. The shrubs and trees and windbreak had gone, and that was that. But we still loved our little house in the Languedoc.

Before winter arrived we started to think about television. I myself had always regarded television as one of the plagues which the Pharaoh of Egypt had been fortunate enough to escape, and I wondered whether it could really be sensible to have one. From what we had seen in the homes of friends in France the programmes were even worse than in England – a fact difficult enough to believe, but none the less undoubtedly true. Almost the whole of the programme on any one of the French channels was either violence, or *film érotique*, or both at once, nine-tenths of the items being American and described almost invariably as *rédiffusion* or *déjà diffusé*. Faced with this endless selection of *déjà vue* we would certainly never have

24

bought a television set in France any more than in England except that we wanted to see the morning weather forecast and watch for the arrow of the Tramontane on the map of prognostications. So, not without misgivings, we selected a modest set at a supermarket and took it to our little house.

When buying a television set in France one has to send in a form which is enclosed in the package, duly completing it before mailing it to a governmental office which controls television licences. The supplier has also to send in a slip showing the sale, so there is no easy means of evading payment. But as usual in France, I examined the small print with a lens and found to my pleasant surprise that there might be a way out. If there were no permanent residents in the house other than one or more males aged sixty-five or over, and women of sixty years or more, and if not one of these dear old things was on even the lowest step of the great French Income Tax ladder – *voilà!* They could have it free.

Back in Jersey once more, we betook us to Crills in St. Helier. Crills had once been the austerely named firm of advocates Crill, Cubitt Sowden and Tomes, a title which carried with it a proper degree of legal pondus. The firm had now shortened its title to Crills, and was mistaken by some for a unisex hairdressing establishment, and by others for a disco. We asked to swear something before a commissioner of oaths, and were shown in to the room of Advocate Gorey, who some years earlier had administered to Ingrid the Oath of Loyalty to Her Majesty which she took upon giving up her Swedish Nationality.

'Hello,' said Advocate Gorey. 'And what can we do for you this time?'

'The French Television is such unadulterated rubbish that we only want to see the weather maps, but not pay.'

The advocate was puzzled. 'Quite so. I don't blame you. But how does it concern me?'

'I wish to swear that I am over sixty-five, and Ingrid over sixty . . .'

'Hard to believe,' said Advocate Gorey, chivalrously.

'. . . and that neither of us pay any French Income Tax whatsoever.'

'Good for you. And you shouldn't either, being domiciled in Jersey. Provided you have no trade or earnings there,' he added. 'Is that all you want to swear?'

'Yes.'

He dictated a statement, which was soon brought through to us on a smartly printed sheet headed 'Declaration of Oath' in expensive-looking Gothic print. He looked it through and then handed me a Bible.

'Place your hand on the Bible and repeat the oath after me.'

I swore the oath.

'That's that,' he said. 'Except that I'm afraid I have to ask you for five pounds. That's the going rate for a tuppenny damn these days, you know.'

We paid up, willingly.

'Now, I will give you a covering translation in French. Then pop round to the French Consul and get the original and the translation certified. And the best of luck.'

The French Consul was as pleasant as could be. We chatted a while about the Languedoc, and the prospects for the year's grape harvest. Then he read our oath and glanced at the translation, signed the original and stamped it over a blue and red *timbre fiscal*.

'I'm afraid I have to ask you for twenty-four pence,' he said apologetically.

I filled in the slip that we had received with the set, claiming exemption from payment for a television licence, and mailed it to the licensing authority along with a copy of the oath. It was with some surprise that I received back an official certificate of exoneration which gave us free television for life. So, after that, we could never complain. Even if the programmes in general were a disgrace to a civilised country, at least we were not paying for them and we could find our enjoyment fully provided in counting the changes of glamourous get-up of the young *météorologistes*, Sophie and Marie-José and Nathalie, who gave us their prognostications every morning at about half past seven.

We returned to Soleil d'Oc for Christmas. We were certainly not in sackcloth even if the van der Born ashes were still around us. The weather was wonderful, and we ate our lunch out-of-doors on Christmas day. Our spirits were high, and we thought everything would turn out well in the end. We even tried to convince ourselves that the new shrubs were growing, and we added a few oleanders and baby pines to the scene. Even if the foreground was a black-and-white patchwork of charred stems and bare limestone rock, the pinewoods across the valley provided a splendid backdrop to the one or two patches of vineyard where there was soil enough for the vines to strike root. Soleil d'Oc was a good place to be, and we were planning a small extra house for family and guests in the corner of the *garrigue*.

Every day we would be up early enough to step out on to the verandah and see the sun rising in golden glory over the vines and the pinewoods beyond them. Ingrid curtseyed as we both gave thanks from hearts filled and flowing over with gratitude.

And then one day in spring it happened again.

This time the fire was much worse in its ravages, and even more ridiculous than that of Jan the schoolmaster in its cause. Our second edition of cypress hedge was struggling to grow, the newest lavenders and cystus planted at the expense of our insurers were taking root well and showing signs of new shoots, when the occupant of the most westerly of all the houses decided to fence his property with wire mesh. He was the only Frenchman in the whole complex, and either he intended to keep rabbits or perhaps he just wanted to erect a stout national barrier to keep out the ubiquitous Dutch. He was slaving away at the unpromising task of driving steel fenceposts in to the stony ground with a heavy sledgehammer, and feeling after a while somewhat exhausted he put down his implement, took out a cigar, lit it, and threw the match down in the dry grass at his feet. The Tramontane was blowing more strongly than ever, as it often did at that time of year, and within seconds a real prairie fire was sweeping down the wind. It missed our house and most of the shrubs, and intrepidly Ingrid pulled out our longest hose and played water on the handsome pine at the end of our land.

Once again, I was away from home when the blaze started. I was attempting a watercolour of the Chateau de Beaufort, near to Olonzac, when I saw the pillar of cloud by day. I raced home to find the whole landscape ablaze. The Bize firemen must have seen the smoke signal from afar, for they were soon on the scene, this time with four vehicles. They realised immediately that it was hopeless to try to tackle the burning brooms and grass and plants of the *garrigue*, and this work they left to those of us who could scoop up buckets of water from the well in our neighbour's vineyard while they concentrated their entire effort on saving the houses down wind.

27

The fire raced for half a mile and destroyed all the Dutch gardens, the flames coming to within three feet of some of the houses, where the pompiers fought them back. Of the seventy graceful and romantic umbrella pines on the heathland, only the one sprayed by Ingrid remained, if somewhat scorched on one side. As for the Frenchman who started the fire, he had disappeared.

Now, it is very easy to pinpoint the starting place of a fire which is only burning in one direction, and it was obvious that the acres of burnt woodland narrowed to a point upwind beside one of the new fence-posts. I fetched my camera, and photographed in detail the exact position where the match had been thrown down. The blaze, of course, could be seen for miles, and after half an hour or more two gendarmes arrived to walk over the scene of devastation in their natty breeches and pill-box caps, shaking their heads and muttering about cretins. Sooty and dirty and sweaty with fighting the blaze, I led them to the starting-point and showed them to an inch where the fencing enthusiast had thrown his match.

'It is good that you have taken photographs,' one of them said, nodding wisely. 'Then the instigator cannot deny responsibility.'

'Exactly,' I said. 'May I assume that this will be a matter of *procès verbal?*'

'*Bien sur.* It is criminal carelessness. He can be held responsible for damages, very great damages. Thousands, tens of thousands of francs.'

'Hundreds of thousands,' his colleague asserted, taking off his cap to wipe his forehead. 'Even millions. To cause a fire of this magnitude can certainly not go unpunished.'

'Good,' I said. 'It could be a lesson to some of those people who start conflagrations.'

'Yes indeed. We shall see if there is any damage to the houses down the far end. It will in any case be very expensive for the incendiary. Such persons are mad, of course.'

The leading officer took out his pad, licked the pencil and began to make notes. He took my name and address. 'Have you yourself suffered damage?'

'Not physically. But the view across the countryside is reduced to ashes, and so are many of our trees and shrubs.'

'*C'est triste.*' He jotted with his pencil. The other officer

28

flicked some offending specks of cinder off his breeches.

'You know the name of the man who started the fire?'

'No. But I have shown you where he lives, and you can easily find out who he is. Besides, you have his car there, and you can identify him from the number, no doubt.'

'It will be very serious for him. There will not only be the criminal charge, but certainly payment in compensation to many many householders. More than a dozen, certainly.'

At this moment the Frenchman who had caused the blaze could be seen returning to his property. The two gendarmes made the motions of tightening their belts and then advanced upon him purposefully, ready to breathe fire and slaughter. But when only a few yards from him they came to a halt, and to my astonishment stood stiffly, and saluted smartly. The individual saluted in turn, rather more casually. Then the three began to chat together in an atmosphere which seemed to me to be unexpectedly relaxed. The cause of the disaster certainly seemed cheerful enough.

After a while the gendarmes saluted again and began to saunter back toward their dark blue Renault Quatre. I cut across to intercept them. I was hot with anger, as well as decidedly dirty.

One of the officers made calming motions with his hand, as though he were stroking a cat.

'There is some mistake,' he said.

'What!'

'He could not have started the fire.'

I was speechless. The other gendarme smiled at me disarmingly. 'Non, non. It is all a great mistake. There will be no report, and no charge of course.'

They had recognised their prey as a high-ranking police officer from Toulouse or Perpignan, and this was his weekend cottage. Naturally, they were frightened of charging him. After all, they had their careers to think of, their wives and children to consider. They did not say all this to me, but I discovered it afterwards.

'One can never be certain where a fire starts . . .'

'Or exactly how . . .'

'*Exactement*. It is impossible to know beyond all possible doubt. So of course we can do nothing. It is most regrettable, and we are very sympathetic, but . . .' He made one of those curious lip noises half-way between spitting and sneezing which is the French term for 'Nothing doing'.

I have never been closer to kicking a policeman than I was at that moment. Indeed, I think I had my foot raised with that unspoken intent. Yet I realised in time that I just could not win. This was France, a glorious country in so many ways, but also one of devious and expert trickery.

'And what about my photographs?'

One of the officers smiled to calm me, but he gave no answer. '*Au revoir, monsieur.* And thank you for your assistance.'

They gave a shadow of a salute, and drove off. I went indoors, had a bath, and then it was tea-time – real tea, English fashion. After 'le fife-au-clock' I wrote out a claim for the second destruction of part of our garden area and posted it to our insurers in Lézignan-Corbières. Two weeks later I received a cheque for the full amount.

The one who suffered the greatest loss through this fire sweeping over the whole extent of the *garrigue* was our builder friend Jan Griffioen. He had managed after a lot of official difficulties to acquire the portion of the heathland not yet built upon, a good area for summer homes and with the pleasant outlook of trees, and a valley, and the pinewoods beyond. He had got building permission, he had marked out the whole area into a dozen or more sites of good size for desirable summer residences, each with a very desirable prospect of highly desirable hills and decidedly desirable woodland. Indeed, we ourselves had paid a small deposit on the two plots immediately ahead of our little house, as we thought that we could well do with more land. Besides, the absence of theoretical Dutchmen was, we considered, even more desirable than their presence.

But now every one of Jan's plots from one end of the area to the other was no more than an undesirable scatter of ashes with the blackened stems of what were once stately umbrella pines to remind people of what the surroundings might have been. The prospects of selling such calcined parcelles were remote indeed.

'Claim on the insurance, Jan,' I said encouragingly. 'They are bound to fork out for the damage you have suffered. I put in a claim and they paid out at once without a murmur. And quite right, too. You have suffered a huge loss on your potential housing here, and you can surely expect them to compensate you.'

Jan thought this a good idea, especially as we all knew how the fire had started. So he carefully drew up a detailed claim and sent it in to the insurers. He had a letter back, to inform him that there was a law that smokers could not be held responsible for setting the place alight.

Tricky, I thought, when he showed it to me. Very astute. But I thought we could call that bluff easily enough.

'Ask them for a copy of the law, Jan,' I suggested. 'A photocopy would do, you could say. Or failing that, the date of the law.' France was well supplied with cryptic notices on walls or fence-posts or public buildings which just baldly stated '*Loi du 7 Septembre 1892*', or something similar, and everyone was supposed to know what it meant.

Jan considered, his head on one side. 'I doubt if they would tell me,' he said. 'And anyway, I don't believe there is such a law, any more than you do, so I wouldn't get an answer if I asked.'

'Well, in that case, why not ask the insurance company how it is they compensated me in full if it is really in the law that smokers can burn down the whole world with impunity, if they feel like it.'

This idea appealed to him, so he wrote to the insurers and asked them just that. How did it come about that they had paid Monsieur Pilkington in full, if such a claim were outside the law?

Again he received a reply. 'The compensation afforded to Monsieur Pilkington was irregular and due to an error of a clerk in the office,' it said baldly.

'That's France,' I said.

Jan laughed bitterly. '*Oui. C'est la belle France. Très belle.* And for that matter *très astucieuse.*'

'Yes, but I would pursue them through your *notaire*, just the same. Get your teeth into them, and don't let go. I will testify for you if you wish, as to the loss you have suffered.'

Jan looked thoughtful, and was evidently considering the implications. 'No,' he said at last. 'I can't do that. Nor could you, in my position.'

He did not need to explain. I could see very well the thoughts that were passing through his mind. He was a foreigner, who was to set about building all these houses the plots of which had been destroyed. He would need to lay on water, and electricity, and drains to the sites before he could even begin to build. Already he had begun some of the necessary road works. If he raised trouble and antagonised people, what would happen? I could imagine it only too clearly. The ground would be declared unsuitable for laying a sewer. Septic tanks could not be used because the strata of rock were inclined in the wrong direction. For some quite unexpected reason it would transpire that drinking water could not be laid on in quantity sufficient for the houses, nor could the electricity substation provide an amperage adequate for that number of dwellings. Even the telephone wires would be subject to some quite unforeseen difficulties. The rating valuation would be found to have been calculated far too low, and the roads now under construction might not be used until a second pavement had been added for the benefit of non-existent pedestrians. Any permit needed before a move could be made in any direction at all would be subject to two or three times the length of the already inexplicable delays. I could see it all perfectly.

'You see,' Jan said, 'this is my living. And this is not Holland. Nor is it England. Not even Jersey.'

'In short, it is France?'

'Yes, it is France. But I love it,' he added with a smile.

I knew that his appraisal of the situation was sensible. 'Come and have a glass of wine,' I suggested.

Ingrid poured out three glasses of the excellent rosé from the Pouzols co-operative, fresh from the fridge.

'To France,' I said.

'To France,' Jan said. 'The land of my choice.'

And we never doubted that it was the land of our choice also, and that of all France it was the Minervois that we loved the most.

☆ ☆ ☆

Before moving in to our little house at Soleil d'Oc we realised that if we were going to be in France for several periods of the year, it would obviously be sensible to have a French bank account instead of relying on cashing cheques or having an endless supply of travellers cheques in our pockets. So, on our way through Paris, we decided to arrange the matter. Not far from the Opéra we noticed the headquarters of the Crédit Lyonnais, and entered through the stately portals.

The Crédit Lyonnais is a nationalised bank which has as its mascot César, an amiable lion that is to be found in an almost life-sized version in the larger branches, and is a favourite for children. ('Mummy, why can't we bank with the C.L.? They have such a cuddly lion there!'). César is an animal that is the epitome of kindness, for he allows the cashiers to smoke like chimneys, so that there is something of a fog at the counter, but César makes up for this to non-smokers by placing big dishes of free toffees on the counter at appropriate times of the year.

We were received with the deference due to eighteenth century oriental ambassadors, and the lady who interviewed us sent for a large-scale map of the southern departments and managed with our help to pinpoint Pouzols upon it. She then made the obviously correct decision that the nearest place of any size was Olonzac, and she checked in the bank's directory that there was a branch of C.L. there. A letter would be sent to the manager of the branch at Olonzac, and if we liked to hand over a cheque for some small amount, say two thousand pounds, then when we returned to France we would find everything ready and waiting for us. The account would be opened, a cheque book would be there, sent by registered post. *Merci, monsieur et madame,* we are enchanted to have your custom. Help yourself to a toffee, and *Bon Voyage!*

When we came back to see how things were progressing at Soleil d'Oc we had enough francs in the handbag to last us for a week or more, but eventually the time came when we needed to stoke up the petty cash. So we drove over to Olonzac. We passed down the main street and noticed the Crédit Agricole, and the BNP, but oddly enough the Crédit Lyonnais eluded us. When we asked people in the shops they appeared puzzled, and with a kindly shake of their heads suggested we should ask somebody else. Which we did, with no result until at last we approached an elderly man sitting on a seat under a plane tree by the market. He was able to point with his stick at a small vacant shop front near the village mini-roundabout. That, he said, was where the Crédit Lyonnais once was, but it had been closed for several years.

The premises were quite obviously empty and there was

nothing inside but the familiar heap of circulars of supermarket bargains optimistically pushed through the letter slit at the bottom of the door, but we could make out the faint remains of the lettering on the facia: Crédit Lyonnais. That was our bank right enough, but its closure some years ago had evidently not yet caused it to be deleted from the list in the Paris head office. César himself was ignorant of its fate. News evidently travelled slowly in the world of banking, or lions.

Our next call was at the Post Office. What, we asked the amiable lady in charge, would happen if, just for the sake of example, a registered letter were to be received at Olonzac for an address which did not exist?

'Ah!' She clicked her teeth. Yes, such things did indeed happen from time to time. There could be errors of address, for example, but it was the duty of the staff of the PTT to serve their customers to the very best of their ability. For that very reason they kept meticulous records – at this point she brought down a child's exercise book from a shelf, blew the dust off, and began to turn the pages.

Could it be that we were referring to a letter from Paris, addressed to the *filiale* of the Crédit Lyonnais in Olonzac? It could? Well, there it was. She turned the book round, and pointed with a pencil. But everyone knew that the branch was closed long ago, many many years. Except the head office? *Oh, la la!*

We asked her what had become of the letter. She pored over the pencilled writing in the copy-book. The letter had been sent on, not back to Paris, but to the nearest branch of the Crédit Lyonnais, *bien sur*.

'And that is . . .?'

'Lézignan-Corbières, Monsieur. It is not far distant.'

In fact, only twenty kilometres. We thanked the post-mistress, praised unstintingly her remarkable practical sense, and set off for Lézignan. Sure enough, our account had been opened, the cheque paid in and cleared, and a *carnet-de-cheques* awaited us. Nobody in the bank had thought of informing us of this change, and we again admired the sagacity of the Olonzac PTT.

Without this forwarding of the mail we might never have discovered Lézignan-Corbières and its Wednesday market which sprawled along the main street, and on the first

Wednesday of the month stretched through the entire town. There one could buy a long, thick sausage of waffle endlessly extruded into a cauldron of boiling fat, or a rotary cultivator, or smoked ham from the heights of the National Park of the Languedoc, or cheeses of endless variety. The less squeamish customers could patronise a lorry with a tank of live trout farmed in the Minervois valleys, point at a victim, have him fished out and clubbed to death on the spot with a pick-axe handle. Rather more sporting perhaps was the system at Olonzac, where on the day of the harvest or wine festival the usually dry fountain, topped with a bold-looking virago of a revolutionary Marianne in breastplate and bosoms, was filled with water circulated by a vintner's irrigation pump. Into the fountain were dumped a few dozen live trout and one might hire a rod for, I think, five francs for one minute. The only successful angler we saw was a boy of five who actually hooked a fish, lifted it flapping on to the roadway and ran off down the street screaming in terror while grandpa took the fish in charge for dinner.

One Wednesday we were off to Lézignan as usual to shop our ham and cheese and bread and asparagus and leeks and olives and apricots and frizzy salad and roast chicken and farm butter and pâté de campagne and quiche and potatoes and radishes and apples and steak and strawberries (if they were locally grown) and mushrooms, and we had promised to be back in the house by eleven o'clock so that a grand-daughter who was studying at Aix could telephone us.

On our way to Lézignan we took the main rocket route as far as where it crossed the canal near Homps, and then turned left by the Ognon brook. At this junction we saw a number of cars parked on the verge, a dozen or two sightseers such as usually collect after an accident, and a couple of gendarmes. We passed them by, vaguely wondering why they were there, as we could see no sign of any crumpled wreckage. We continued to Lézignan, shopped the whole of our list in the weekly market as intended, and then set out on our return. But when we came up to the main road again by the Ognon brook the exit was closed.

'*On ne passe pas,*' said one of the gendarmes briefly, like a general at Verdun. There was now a rather larger crowd of hangers-about, we noticed.

... that most popular of French sports ...

But we were only going home, I said. Just a kilometre or so over the hill.

Mais non. The road was closed, and that was that. *On ne passe pas.* All the side roads between Carcassonne to the west and Béziers to the east were closed. *On ne passe pas.* It was as clear as that. One might not enter the main road.

'Is it President Mitterand?' I knew he liked to travel in style.

The gendarme laughed at our astonishing ignorance. 'No. It is the Tour de France!'

In the greatest event of the year of that greatest and most popular of French sports, the bicycle race, with nose to handlebar, shirt and pants plastered with advertisements of all the sponsors from chocolate bars to rubber tyres, the great swarm of cyclists was passing by Carcassonne and following the main road which also happened to be the only way to Soleil d'Oc. Nobody – probably not even the President himself – could be allowed to obstruct the triumphal way. Not so much as a pop-popping moped could desecrate the route. Only, of

36

course, the painters employed by the 'red' trades union had been allowed the previous day to paint the initials CGT in huge letters on the tarmac once every few hundred yards, but I had been ignorant of why these letters should have suddenly appeared.

I looked at my watch. Half past ten. I asked the gendarmes what time the road would be reopened. About midday, they thought. Maybe later. But certainly not until all the riders had passed. So there was no chance at all of reaching home by eleven o'clock for the telephone call. None at all, unless . . .

We turned our little Renault Quatre and raced back to Argens with its curious chateau standing on a mound and overlooking the canal. We crossed the waterway, and followed a country road that ran parallel with it to Roubia. Turn left, turn right, and a minor road wound to and fro between the vineyards and *pinède* to cross the row of chalky hills.

Down the other side and just short of a ruined farm there was a rough track which seemed to lead to one of the cabins where, before the days of tractors, the family and their horse would spend their sacred hour of lunchtime. I recognised the little building because I had seen it in the distance when I had explored the hills on foot while trying to discover a pleasant route for a round walk of three or four hours to suit our more energetic visitors.

Bumping along the track we eventually came to an impassable ditch. There was nothing to be done but to turn and go back to the road and try again. But time was running out. The next vineyard track served us better, and hurrying along it for some way we came at last to a *chemin* which led to the cabin and turned behind it into a lane which climbed up toward the pines and was obviously suitable for vehicles. There, another *chemin* curved away round the edge of a bump in the hillside, then narrowed and descended westward. I knew exactly where I was now, and I turned into a sandy track which crossed a brambly ravine on a small concrete bridge. Two more minutes, and I knew that the main road was just ahead, round the corner, behind a clump of Spanish broom. It was now five minutes to eleven, and if we could sneak quietly out into the roadway nobody would see us, I was sure, and we could reach the telephone in time.

Just as I was congratulating myself on having found the way

37

there was a roar of motorcycles, and a herd of police surged past. They were followed by a loudspeaker van, several cars of journalists and trucks with television crews, a placard lorry advertising coffee, an open car from which free paper hats advertising the local paper of the department could be thrown to children, a van displaying a brand of washing machine and another shouting through a loudspeaker the unbelievable whitening quality of a brand of detergent, with a free trip for two to the Caribbean thrown in if we were lucky. The Tour de France had arrived in all its salesmen's splendour.

I edged up to the road and looked to the left. The string of traffic extended up to where the road turned a bend toward Olonzac, and further than that I could not see. But there seemed to be a little space between the van of the '*Midi Libre*' and the truck following, which carried a load of spare cycles. Fifty yards of space, perhaps, not more. And the column was travelling at a considerable speed. I revved up the engine and as *Midi Libre* came abreast of us, with flying gravel and a squeal of tyres the little Renault shot out into the road.

We were in the race.

We had not far to go now. Soon I could see the Soleil d'Oc lane at the foot of the hill. There was a gathering of the Occers standing in the end of the small road and a gendarme barring the way to keep them from straying out. But we had no chance to slow down without being bumped from the rear. I turned on the headlights and the flasher for turning right, put my hand on the horn and swung in between the reflector posts. The young gendarme jumped smartly to the grass verge, the assembled Dutch fell back on either side as we swept through and up the hill to disappear over the top of the ridge. We were safely out of the race, and home.

Soon after we reached the house the telephone rang. We absorbed the grand-daughterly news and then hurried out to the shrubby area behind the house, from which we had an excellent view down to the main road. The string of cars and trucks of the pressmen and television and advertisers was still passing, but soon there came a gap. Then a police car, and a few motorised gendarmes. Behind them, deep in the fumes of the exhaust-laden air, came the pack of cyclists, a compact mass, sweaty and dusty. One of them must have been a Dutchman, because we heard the Occers at the estate entrance raise a cheer.

One or two laggards, a score of cars with spare bikes and wheels on the roof, a few large trucks belonging to cycle manufacturing companies, a final police car, and the gendarme down at the entrance adjusted his cap, took up his noddy-bike and set off for home. The Tour de France had passed, like the King of Glory, on its way. And that, I thought, was that.

But now a new invasion was in sight. Mile upon mile of cars, trucks, petrol bowsers, pantechnicons, cement-mixers, wine-tankers, a tourist bus or two, tractors, caravans, market vans, a yacht on a *convoi-exceptionnel* transporter, bumper to bumper they extended as far as one could see. Every side road for forty miles had been sealed off for two or three hours, and now at last the traffic was free to pour out into the main road and crawl along at the speed of the slowest in the wake of the cavalcade, and in a traffic jam that was to be repeated elsewhere day after day throughout the week.

This adventure of finding the cross-country tracks which were just passable for a car, albeit a small one, was soon to turn out to be very useful. One morning in the late autumn we were glorying in the unbroken sunshine and taking a leisurely glass of *grenache* on our terrace before lunch. We were looking out across the woodlands of the minor hills towards the hazy form of the Mont d'Alaric in the Corbières, when I noticed a little wisp of smoke at the edge of one of the vine-fields just across the valley. Evidently a wine-grower was burning up the accumulated wind-blown leaves, but with my field-glasses I could see that nobody was actually present and attending to the bonfire. I was still scanning the area to see where the man might be, when the flames shot up, first climbing a pine at the edge of the woodland and then leaping from tree to tree like a giant squirrel.

I quickly phoned the worthy pompiers at Bize and gave them the exact location. But it was not at all easy to find a route to the copse, now well ablaze, and as I happened to know all the vineyard and woodland *chemins* intimately I told them that I would wait in our little white Renault at the layby opposite the entrance to Soleil d'Oc, and from there I would lead the way.

This time we had three engines and a water tanker bumping over the rough paths, and I escorted them to the front of the flames and prudently parked our car on the up-wind side. The battle began.

By mid-afternoon the fire was finished. So was the wood-land, and what had remained of our view.

The gendarmes came once again to stroll over the land and survey the scene of desolation. It transpired that a wine-grower had lit the fire and then driven home the twenty-five kilometres to Narbonne for lunch. One of the gendarmes clicked his tongue and said it was a cretinous act. Of course, there would be a criminal charge made.

I smiled, but said nothing. This was France.

3

The Real Consorts Property

Home again in Jersey we began to wonder what we should do about the changes at Soleil d'Oc, and what sort of a future the place had for us, if any. We loved the little house, we had made a good second home of it, and we found the surroundings of countryside and nature very much to our taste. But the fact remained that short of an earthquake, Soleil d'Oc had by now had as much in the way of disasters as would satisfy most people for a lifetime.

Actually, and quite unknown to us at that time, it had had even more, although in this particular instance it did not affect us. For most of the winter months the twenty-eight houses scattered around the heathland were not lived in, so the complex provided an excellent hunting-ground for minor thieves who were not after big game but more inclined to the simple things of life – bedding, clothes, a supply of canned food, and perhaps a radio and television set or two to while away the dark evenings between robberies. Early in the New Year twenty-seven houses were broken into. Only one was not, and that was Number Twenty.

We had no doubt at all that this was because of our alarm system. This consisted in having a blue metal alarm box situated high on the outside wall with the word ALARM painted on it in white. We reckoned that even the most cretinous of French thieves could guess what the word implied, and evidently we were right. Our house was spared, and undoubtedly that was because of the alarm box. Which happened to be empty. All we lost was our outdoor thermo-meter.

We were so uncertain about the future of our little house as a place where we would still want to spend our ever-increasing retirement holiday time that I pored over the yellow pages of the Aude telephone directory and extracted the names of twenty-four *agences immobilières* – though I skipped the madame who had shown us the properties near Carcassonne. I wrote to each of them, enclosing a carefully and clearly set-out list of our requirements. I posted the letters, and waited. Of the twenty-four, twenty-one sent no reply of any kind. Of the three who bothered to answer the letter, two sent details of time-sharing sea side flats at Gruissan and Narbonne Plage. Only one paid the slightest attention to the carefully worked-out schedule we had submitted. That was Immobilier le Grix.

It was Madame le Grix who wrote back, and she took the trouble to write a sensible and friendly letter in English. Enclosed with it were details of three properties which she thought might be suitable. We looked over the details and decided that the first thing to be done was to satisfy ourselves as to whether Soleil d'Oc was ruined for ever, or whether perhaps the spring rains might already have caused the charred wilderness to blossom like a rose.

On Easter Monday I flew to Paris and caught the sleeper to Narbonne in order to make an appraisal. It only took me a moment to decide. The landscape was utterly ruined. That there would ever be more than a covering of scrub during our lifetime was not likely, and for a few years there would not even be that.

I set off to inspect the le Grix offerings. The first was in a sensible little village in an acceptable area of the Minervois, at the foot of the hills which led up to the Montagne Noire, and not very far from our shopping town of Olonzac. It had a garden, the house itself was a solidly built villa of standard design, and it was close to its neighbours, all of whom, I was sure, would be Dutch. Cesseras I knew to be virtually a Dutch province, and we wanted to live not in Overijssel or Gelderland or among Amsterdammers, but in France.

Next I inspected a house above Siran, another village in the same area. I could see the attraction of this property, but it was definitely not for us, as it was on the top of a bare mountain across which the wind whistled so violently that I wondered that the roof was still on the bungalow. I only ventured within half a mile of it. There was no other farm or house within sight, and I wondered also if one would really be able to stand up in the winter gales if one ventured outside the front door. I also doubted whether they would ever be able to find a customer for such a wind-raked spot, but perhaps one day some scientist might turn up who wanted to study the possibility of generating electricity by the power of the Tramontane.

The last of Madame le Grix's selection was described by her as 'The Real Consorts Property'. I wondered as I drove toward the village where it was situated, whether we would be suitable inhabitants for premises which I assumed to be more appropriate for Prince Albert. The house was at Montouliers, and the page describing its virtues gave very little information but included a photocopy of a small photograph which showed a number of shapes which I took to be trees, and a black smudge in a greyish surface further to the left.

I approached the place from the direction of Bize, a village on the River Cesse which had been the subject of one of my earlier watercolours. The road led up through scattered woodland and below a scarp of rock to cross an area of earth as bright red as the Colorado Provençal near Roussillon. Then it swung to the left a little, levelled off, and turned a corner to open up a startling view of what must certainly be one of the most charmingly situated villages of all the Languedoc. St. Guilhem le Desert claims to have first place, and I think perhaps rightly so; but I would have no doubts about awarding second place to Montouliers.

The road began to descend a little, curving between vineyards to reach the edge of a steep-sided little valley. Across it and to the left was something that I immediately recognised as the grey mass of the illustration on the le Grix information sheet, a splendid, massive bulk of limestone cliff in greyish white and orange, and at the bottom of the crag the black smudge revealed itself to be a cave. I stopped the car and stood at the edge of the road, looking across the *vallon* to the most alluring and wonderfully situated house I had ever seen. There was no doubt about its identity. It was the Real Consorts Property. I did not immediately drive round and up through the village to inspect it. There was no need. I looked at my watch, made my way to the tiny village post office and phoned our Jersey number. There was an hour of time difference between France and Jersey, so it was not yet eleven o'clock

43

... a splendid, massive limestone cliff, and at the
bottom a cave

there. It was just possible that Ingrid could have time to catch
the Paris plane.

'Leave everything. Come at once. Jersey European to Paris,
than the usual flight to Montpellier,' I said. (We were always
economical in telephone talk.) 'I'll pick you up at Narbonne
station about six o'clock.'

'But what . . .?' Ingrid began. Then she stopped. She knew it
must be something important if I was so reckless as actually to
use the telephone at all. 'I'm coming,' she said. 'You must have
found something.'

'Yes. The Real Consorts Property!'

I left the post office, but I still did not visit the premises.

Even if the house should have an Emmentaler loo, a mere
hole in a flat surface, that could easily be put right. There was
nothing that could not be fixed if need be. The house had a
superb position. It was better by far than our wildest dreams of
a *pied en France*.

My next action was to phone le Grix and tell him we were interested and ask him to put the property on hold. He agreed, and promised to come up to the house next morning at ten o'clock, when the necessary negotiations could take place. Meanwhile, he would ask the lady who lived there for a final and definite figure.

When Ingrid arrived that evening at Narbonne I collected her and drove her by the St. Pons road from the town in order to approach the village as I had done myself, from the direction of Bize. Coming round the curve from the area of red earth and past the pinewood and the vineyards, I slowed and finally stopped above the *vallon* with its little vegetable plots at the bottom, and a vineyard spilling down the slope on the nearer side. Across the ravine another and larger vineyard sloped down toward a line of elderly olive trees which edged a brambly tangle of thicket that concealed the slight trickle of a stream. At the top of those vines a very minor road, a *chemin*, climbed gently toward the village, and across it above a long stone wall stood a group of stout blue cypresses, a slender blue spruce, and a number of other handsome conifers overshadowed by a gigantic umbrella pine. Nestling at the back of this plantation was a house with full-length windows behind a railed terrace. It had the appearance of looking at us out of the eyes of its small dormer windows as though appealing to us to make its closer acquaintance.

'What do you think of that?'

'You mean . . . that house? Why, it's . . . it's . . . I don't think I've ever seen a place as beautiful!'

'It's ours. Or will be in a few months, with luck. Le Grix is coming up in the morning to arrange the contract.'

Next morning we drove over from the desolation surrounding our poor little house at Soleil d'Oc which had brought us so much happiness, up through the village street of Montouliers, down the *chemin*, and into the curving gravelled drive which led up to the side of the house. The owner was waiting for us, and when le Grix introduced us we realised that the correct name of the property was *Les Cactus*, and its very appropriate title in Madam le Grix's letter was merely her English for what might more commonly be rendered: 'The property of Monsieur and Madame Real'.

Monsieur Real, we discovered, was no more. He had been a

something-or-other on the mechanical side of the aircraft industry in Toulouse. He had evidently been a very practical man, and a compulsive wall builder too. Altogether there were at least a hundred yards of stone wall in various parts of the domaine, some of it fifteen feet high. Many of the stones must have weighed more than a hundredweight apiece, and he had hauled them in from all over the countryside and constructed the walls single-handed. Madame Real told us that it was she who built all the walls, a statement vigorously denied by everyone else in the village of Montouliers, who assured us that it was he and not she who had been the constructor, and that he was also responsible for the high retaining wall at the back of the church. From photographs I could see that Monsieur Real was a man of large proportions, especially round the equator, and if he died suddenly of a heart attack I suspected that the lifting and placing of a few hundred tons of rock might have had something to do with it.

Madame Real now lived alone in the house, which she obviously loved. It had been the family holiday home, and the Reals had built it in 1967 in the position which then, as now, was unique. On the west it was sheltered by the towering bulk of the cliff from the strongest puffs of the Tramontane, the wind which was represented on French TV weather maps by the left-hand of the two arrows which made their appearance on appropriate days – and which in the case of the Tramontane was whenever the difference in temperature between the mountain tops and the lower lying areas was at a maximum. That was, of course, during the spring and the autumn, according to the rules, but also in high summer and mid-winter according to our own experience. In other words, you could never know when it was coming, and even the omniscience of the forecasters could sometimes be wildly adrift. The other arrow, to the right of the Tramontane, was the famous Mistral (or Master Wind), a wind we recalled only too well from boating days, and which blew due south and then turned somewhat along the coast towards Corsica, whereas the Tramontane was shown as blowing from the north-west, which on the whole it did.

On top of this cliff and very close to its edge stood three large umbrella pines, handsome trees indeed, and we noticed that two of them were held back by massive steel cables, attached to

46

some sort of anchor, we presumed. A flight of steps (another piece of Real stone construction) led up to a paved area surrounded by a formidable fence of wire mesh, which looked like a small concentration camp. It contained two mighty kennels, one build out of concrete *in situ*, and the other a massive wooden one. These had been for the hunting dogs, which we presumed must have been of more than average size. They had their exercise ground within the wire, and a floodlight on a mast to give them plenty of illumination at night. Presumably this was so that they could read in bed, because more than ninety per cent of the sensory input of a dog comes through the nose and not through the eyes, but up to now no olfactory enhancers seem to have been invented. The dogs which lived in this compound had now gone, leaving their homes behind them.

Above and behind all this was a hay-field orchard with a scatter of non-playing trees of fig and quince and cherry, and to the right the vineyard sloped down gently toward the entrance drive. It was not large, only perhaps a couple of hundred vines of various kinds, but to us it was thrilling. Our own vineyard! We felt like infant Mouton Rothschilds.

Apart from the specimen trees below the terrace there were some two hundred others on the domaine, which straggled away around the corner beyond the cave. Some of these were elms which had caught the familiar Dutch Elm disease, others were mainly various kinds of pines, and there were also a number of olives and a scattering of almonds.

Much the largest tree was the huge umbrella pine at the corner of the terrace, and although it had lost nearly one third of its height in a hurricane it was still by far the most majestic pin parasol that I had ever seen. It was obviously a survivor of times long before the Real era, and they had cleverly incorporated it as a feature of the lay-out, building another flight of stone steps to pass round behind it to the lower area, where once there had apparently been a *potager* or vegetable patch belonging to somebody in the village. There the Reals had put four circles of scrubby cotoneasters, which encircled the bases of three handsome trees, one of which was the fine blue spruce. A fourth tree had evidently died, so one of the circles was empty; but the result was that we had a magnificent view right across the plain to distant Narbonne and the coastal headland of La Clape. As soon as we saw the circles we decided that it would be a great improvement to grub them out and replace them by that rather useless curiosity beloved of all Britons, a genuine lawn.

Madame Real was small, easy-going, and ladylike in a somewhat tweedy way. She could have been the wife of an English squire, and at the moment she was attended by a son of such Mediterranean appearance that we wondered if he were a Corsican or Greek. He in turn had in attendance a glamorous, sylph-like and scantily bikinied girl who reclined languidly in a hammock, and in spite of her superlatively displayed figure, must have been the mother of the three-year-old boy who was continually following his grandmother around as she showed us the domaine.

The young couple paid no attention to us at all. They did not even stand up. Their thinly veiled hostility was, of course, easily understood. They loved the place too in their own way, and maybe it held childhood memories also for the young man. So it was natural enough that neither of them was inclined to welcome with courtesy, let alone enthusiasm, the arrival of two outsiders who might take the place from them – and who were foreigners also.

Madame was warm, friendly, and courtesy itself. And no wonder, for *Les Cactus* had been on the market for a year and a half already and yet remained unsold. The obvious conclusion was that the price she expected was far too high, and le Grix told us that he had continually been telling her that she would have to bring the price down. By now the figure had fallen by more than two-fifths, and Ingrid and I took a walk down the drive while le Grix got her to confirm the final definite figure which she would accept.

Then we returned to the living-room, sat down with her, and performed all the familiar *lu et approuvé* and *bon-pour-achat* ritual.

Madame Real signed the contract, le Grix witnessed the signatures, and we sat back.

All of us were thoroughly pleased. She had sold her house at long last, we had bought the place that was already of our heart's delight, Robert le Grix could pocket a handsome commission – at a rate which would astonish agents in Britain – and the two notaries would soon be able to get down to the intricacies of preparing the *acte* and getting ready to accept without a blush their fees.

It was a brilliant morning, but being early April there was a freshness in the air, and Madame Real had a fine fire blazing in the wide, open hearth of the living-room. It was an ingenious fireplace, because it was deep from back to front and had fire-dogs (which she removed as soon as we had left) and a hollow steel back which connected with an air-space under the floor, the other end of which was open to the outside through a grating set in the ground at the foot of the house wall. The air in the steel jacket was heated, rose, and came out into the room through a decorative grating above the mantelpiece in the broad chimney breast. Madame was very proud of this device and she led me over to feel for myself the strong current of heated air.

No wonder the room was so pleasantly warm, she said. Almost too warm – that was why she had opened the French windows. But in any case it was pleasant to let some sunshine in, was it not? Besides, it seemed such a shame to shut out all the wonderful spring warmth; sun through glass was a poor substitute for the real thing, wasn't it? The living-room of nearly five hundred square feet had three pairs of full-length glazed doors to the outside and another to the hall. It was the hall doors and one of the outside pairs that she had so magnanimously opened for the sake of the sun.

Madame Real appeared to suffer from a terror of burglars, and that was why, she explained, she preferred a bedroom with no windows, so that she might not be spied upon. The path coming up to the house from the lane and passing up the steps by the pin parasol was obstructed by a mass of cut thorny branches and barbed wire; the approach along the level from the copse at the entrance was likewise protected by a barbed wire entanglement, and even the access from where the *potager* had been was made impassable (as she thought) with thorny bushes. Along the top of the wall down the lane the spiky flesh of the barbary fig cacti from which the house took its name defied the tramps who, she said, slept regularly in the cave. I learned in the village that they had indeed done so in former times, but by now tramps were rare. Social Security had provided them with the basic needs of life.

While we were discussing the formalities of the sale, I

noticed a note written on half a sheet of paper and left on the sideboard. It was a pathetic appeal to *cambrioleurs* to leave her in peace. Why burgle her house and not others? Be kind, please, and go elsewhere.

Madame Real saw that I was reading the message. Three times, she said, they had broken into her house. Yes, three times. Once they had even taken her bedstead.

I was uncertain how much to believe, but I made suitably sympathetic tongue-clicks and put on an expression like Toulouse-Lautrec's sad portrait of a dismal dog. At the same time I realised that one of my first tasks would be to demolish the defences. Except, of course, for the cacti.

Madame Real then opened the door of the particularly hideous Monsieur Meuble sideboard built in the horrid sham-antique style of the middle-of-the-century French furnishing. She took out a half empty bottle of muscat and four glasses. We raised them to seal the contract in *amitié*.

The telephone rang. A male voice was on the line. Madame listened, and gave a sort of gasp.

'*Mais c'est vendue, monsieur,*' she said. '*Oui, oui, oui. C'est trop tard.*' She added that she was *désolée*, then put down the receiver. It was the gentleman from Rouen, she told le Grix. It was two weeks since he had looked over the house and had thought about it, but the contract was signed, was it not?

Le Grix nodded, and said something about people never being able to make up their minds. Obviously it was not a customer he himself had introduced.

Madame Real would probably have netted ten thousand francs more on the sale if the man from Rouen had been quicker, but now at least she had the certainty of the money and she did not complain. And I myself realised that only Ingrid's alacrity in coming down to southern France at a moment's notice had secured for us the happy place which was soon to bring us more delight than we could ever have imagined.

The period of incubation now began. From time to time we drove over from Soleil d'Oc to take stock of the situation in the vineyard or the orchard, or to ask madame's permission to measure one of the rooms, or bring Jan Griffioen to puzzle over the difficulties he might encounter when the transfer of the title was completed and he could begin to make the transformations

50

we had been planning in our minds. At first, Madame would give us the friendliest and most smiling of welcomes, but each time we saw her she seemed to us to become more and more withdrawn, her natural charm of manner less obvious, her happiness at having at last disposed of the property clouded. Not that she was anything but polite; it was just that she was not quite the same endearing lady that she had been when first we met her. Summer was here, the vines were shooting, the rosy buds peeping from the bracts of the two giant oleanders she had planted many years ago below the terrace, and we sympathetically attributed her decline to her feeling that all this beauty would soon no longer be hers.

When at last the *acte* was signed, we felt a surge of relief. The keys were handed over, and Madame Real removed to Toulouse, leaving behind her twenty-nine empty wine bottles, a wheelbarrow, the broken back axle of a car, an old rake, a shovel, and a worn pair of vine-clippers.

4

The New Arrivals

With the house now legally ours, it was not just a case of moving in. There were necessary changes to be made, and we reckoned to have enough work for Jan Griffioen and his merry men to last them for two or three months. Some of these changes were what Jan called 'just a matter of taste', and this taste sometimes reflected nothing more than Anglo-Swedish obstinacy over matters which to the French were relatively unimportant.

Such as the toilet. The Reals had been content with a loo which was certainly one degree up on an Emmenlater, but had neither lighting, nor window, nor ventilation of any kind. It was a kind of closed box in the corner of the bathroom, rather like the cell into which psychologists sometimes shut people for reasons which are not altogether obvious. Just as remarkable was madame's personal bedroom, which was at the end of the entrance hall, and had only a pale gleam of light borrowed from the hall through amber-tinted glass panels. There was no window of any kind, not so much as an air-brick ventilator. It was airtight, and no doubt she had considered it burglar-tight as well, so we had to break through the exterior wall to install a broad window, adding instead of a bedstead a proper modern kitchen with a door to the dining area. The view from the window only extended for less than three feet before reaching a blank wall, this being the exterior of the wine-store which was built into the rising ground behind. But a large wine-store was hardly necessary in a place such as Montouliers, where nobody could cultivate anything other than vines, so we reduced it to a size adequate for about two hundred bottles and sloped the rest back as a series of small terraces reaching up to the domaine of the vanished hunting-dogs, so providing a wonderful display of flowers which was more stimulating for whoever happened to be doing the cooking than a blank wall of granite and limestone.

Other rooms had to be turned around, and stripped of that particularly horrid kind of wallpaper which is a delight, it seems, to the French eye – that is, heavy patterns in black and off-chocolate brown.

As soon as we arrived to take stock of the general state of things we turned the corner of the house to walk up the flight of stone steps to the domaine of the hunting-dogs. These steps had been overshadowed by three very fine umbrella pines near the edge of the cliff above. Now we saw that two of these beautiful, elegant trees were no longer there. A pair of broad and newly sawn stumps was all that was left of them. The third tree, which did not really overshadow the house, was still there, but the others . . .

Our first reaction was one of fury; but then we understood that Madame had been fearful that the two trees set right on the edge of the cliff and held back by stout steel cables to some sort of anchors in the land behind them might be pushed over by a violent storm and come crashing down upon the house, demolishing in one vicious gust her dream of receiving the purchase price. It was a risk she dared not take. Cut down the trees and let the purchaser go hang – that was the obvious solution.

And then our righteous wrath abated. The two big pines would not only have been an ever-present menace, but they also shaded that side of the house to such an extent that one would have needed to have the light on in the bedroom even in the daytime. Now the daylight was admitted – and our cursings turned to blessings.

Our autumn was one of coming and going. *Thames Commodore* was still lying at the canal junction, where she provided an excellent hotel annexe for friends who came to visit us. Her far-ranging cruising days were now over, and she was hopefully awaiting a suitable customer who would buy her. We still had Soleil d'Oc as well, and we had no intention of disposing of that little house which, if one turned ones back on the ash of the countryside, was still a happy place, until we could move in finally at Montouliers.

There was plenty to occupy us. Tiles had to be chosen for

bathrooms and kitchen, and the lay-out of the cooking area had to be finalised with the kitchen installers. The workshop had to be fitted out and equipped, and any necessary furniture for the house itself had to be chosen, most of it in Spain, where an excellent furniture shop was only an hour and a half distant, outside Figueras.

We already had experience of French furniture shops. There were chains of them across the country – Monsieur Meuble, Conforama, Euromeuble, and others. To enter any one of them was the same experience, for they all stocked similar if not identical lines of what in Britain would have been mock-Tudor, bogus-Victorian and sham-Renaissance mass-produced horror. The worst department of all was the *luminaires*. One had only to enter a French café with its frightful strip-lighting darkened with the excrement of flies to realise that there was not much taste where illumination was concerned.

Nevertheless, beds were necessary in Soleil d'Oc – the Dutch had had only collapsible camp-beds – and we needed also one or two other essential pieces. So we went to Revel, a curious and symmetrically designed town at the far side of the Montagne Noire, renowned as a great centre of furniture made of wood from the nearby forests. We imagined it to be a sort of French High Wycombe.

In fact, Revel consisted almost entirely of furniture shops, and many of them sold the same hideous items that one could find in Monsieur Meuble and his rivals. But others had real, genuine hand-made, well-crafted and tastefully designed items of every description and at prices correspondingly high. A few smaller workshops specialised in top quality reproductions of Louis Quatorze and Seize, and we found one young man at work upon an exquisite bureau, part of an order from one of the great ducal mansions in England which would keep him busy with marquetry and inlay for the next three years. If he were given photographs of some priceless piece in the Victoria and Albert he could produce an identical item and defy anyone to tell at sight which was the original and which his new creation.

So the visit to Revel was at least stimulating. And in one of the larger shops we found a fine, sturdy, excellent short-legged table, just the thing to have in front of the sofa. This sofa we had of course acquired at the IKEA store in Marseille, where good taste and quality could be relied upon.

We bought the table, and paid. 'We can take it in the car,' I said. 'If there is somebody who can take it down the stairs for us . . .'

'*Mais non-non-non-non.*' It was necessary to give it a final polish in the workshop. Madame would see that it was delivered to us. *Pas de problème.*

'Tomorrow?'

That would not be possible.

'Next week?'

'Of course.' We understood that there was no need at all to break our heads about the table. It would arrive.

Next week passed. We phoned madame, who was desolate. There had been trouble with the truck, but that had now been arranged. Why not tomorrow? Oh, la la! She did not know what plans the driver had.

Another week passed, and a month. Then two months. Always when we telephoned to Revel there was some good reason why transport had not been possible.

At the end of three months I wrote a letter asking for the price of the table to be remitted at once by cheque. Next morning the table arrived.

Much the same happened with the beds which we selected at Carcassonne. No, one could not have the beds on view in the showroom. Similar beds would be brought from the store and delivered, probably this week. None came, and after weeks of evasion we happened to pass the shop and I went in and asked for the money back.

Consternation. Money? They were not allowed to pay money out of the till. No, a cheque was not possible either as cheques had to be signed by a director.

'Fetch him,' I said with determination. Years of obstruction by frontier officials when voyaging into France by canal or river had steeled my determination. Stand fast and demand – that was the only way to deal with the French subordinate.

'Fetch the director?'

'Yes, at once. If he must sign the cheque.'

'Now?'

'Yes. Go and get him.'

'Perhaps tomorrow . . .'

'Now.'

The assistant went off and after a while returned to say, as we expected, that the director could not be found. Maybe he had gone to Toulouse.

I asked for paper and pencil, wrote a demand for the money and got the assistant to promise that he would give the message to the director at nine next morning and post the cheque before midday. Then we left, an example of the incomprehensible impatience of people from the land of perfidy.

At nine o'clock next morning a pleasant van driver knocked on our door at Soleil d'Oc to say he had two beds for us. And so he had. Luckily we took off the wrapping of one before he had turned his van to leave. They were beds right enough, painted a ghastly, nightmare hue of brilliant orange, and certainly not ours. Another week, and I drove to Carcassonne and said I would sit in the shop until we had the beds or the money. And lo and behold, a smiling director came to tell us he was desolate that there had been an error, but our beds had now been found. A thousand regrets, but the beds would be sent shortly.

'Now.' I said. 'Or a cheque in full.'

'Now?'

'Now.' And we got the beds.

After these experiences of prevarication by French furniture shops we much preferred to find what we needed at Decor Mobel of Figueras in Spain, and IKEA in Marseille, or – when we were en route from Jersey – at their branch at Evry outside Paris. We were not surprised to find all the IKEA shops well patronised by French families, who for the first time in their lives could see really top quality modern furniture and know that it was there to take away – now.

That was supposed also to be the principle of a large cash-and-carry chain of French furniture stores, and as they had mattresses of good quality to take away we thought it sensible to buy a pair at their branch outside Narbonne, rather then carry such bulky objects a hundred miles in the car. Sure enough, we found what we wanted, paid with our Carte Bleue, and were given the docket to take round to the delivery door at the rear. And then the bell rang.

'You must leave, monsieur et madame.' It was the holy hour of lunch.

'But . . . our mattresses?'

'This afternoon. We re-open at three.'

56

'At three! And what do you expect us to do for the next three hours?'

The obvious answer was of course: have lunch. But the assistant merely shrugged and muttered something non-committal. It was not his business how we occupied ourselves.

I went to the cash desk. 'Please give me back my Carte Bleue slip,' I said.

'That is impossible, monsieur.'

'Then give me the amount in cash. I am not going to sit on the doorstep for three hours.'

'We cannot refund you the money, monsieur. The till is closed.'

'O.K. Then I shall wait.' I sat down in one of their hideous leather armchairs. 'This is a cash-and-carry store. You have taken the money. I shall leave when I have the goods, or the money back. *Pas de discussion!*' I crossed my legs and reclined in a pose of relaxation.

Consternation. The manageress was consulted. Departing customers looked at me sympathetically, wondering if I had been taken ill. Ingrid smiled reassuringly at everybody, including the manageress. The assistant who had served us looked at his watch. He was hungry.

'You cannot wait here,' the manageress said in a honeyed voice, giving me a soothing smile. 'You must leave . . .'

'*Bien sur.* With the goods.' I did not move.

Now began frantic ringings on the intercom telephones. Quick conversations. Frowns. Clicking of teeth. Gestures of despair. The security man by the door was jangling his keys and the cashier was putting on lipstick.

A sudden gasp from the girl at the phone. She whispered something to her superior, who came over to me smiling happily.

'Monsieur. One of the warehouse staff is still on the premises. He is willing to carry down the mattresses to the delivery door. If you drive round to the rear you may have them now.'

I smelled a possible trap. Get this awkward customer outside and shut the door behind him? I stood up, thanked the manageress for her help, and then asked her to declare unequivocally that our goods were there and would be handed over without any nonsense.

She did. They were. We gave the warehouseman five francs and apologised for delaying his lunch.

He was pleased. And so were we.

Even though we could not move in to our new home because works were still in progress, we had other things to occupy us beside the furnishing. The whole domaine had to be taken care of, with its fruit trees, the oleanders and all such plants as made southern France so beautiful. There was the wine harvest too, or more correctly the grape harvest, for we had not the face to take our humble offering down to the village co-operative to add to the EEC's vast lake of surplus plonk. On the eve of our next departure to Jersey we picked all the bluish wine grapes and carefully laid the bunches in boxes after we had proudly weighed them. The total came to just over eighteen kilos, and of course we were pleased. But with proper care and spraying and fertilising the yield from that same patch of vines the following year was to be more than thirty times as great.

We returned to Soleil d'Oc for the last time in November, to find that the *loirs* had been having a wonderful time during our absence. The *loir* was something quite new to both of us, for it is not found at all either in Britain or in Scandinavia, and even if it ranks as a kind of a dormouse it is not at all the same as the sleepy and rather fat creature which shared the tea-party with Alice and the hatter. There were no *loirs* in Montouliers either, and I was soon to find that the people there had neither seen nor heard of them, but at Soleil d'Oc they were a real pest. However much one might try to get rid of them they always returned, because they had an excellent undisturbed breeding-ground in one of the houses which was otherwise uninhabited.

One of the original purchasers of a plot of land was a Dutch airline pilot. He was awarded a site on the edge of a steep *vallon*, and there his house was built. But it proved a perfect example of the folly of choosing a wrong foundation as set out in Luke 6, for unknown to the buyer the house was placed on a built-up pile of spoil, a mass of sand and gravel from the excavation of other sites. It was not even necessary for a storm to rage to bring disaster. Aided only by its own modest weight, the house began to sink at one edge and then to fall apart. There were cracks several inches wide in some of the walls and the place was not habitable at all. Even if it had been, it could at any

Eliomys quercinus, the animal
the French call a *loir*

moment have fallen over and disappeared into the valley below. We were sorry for the pilot who had paid for such a useless ruin to be built, and he had no redress, for the man he naturally wished to sue was bankrupt.

The walls of this house were partly insulated with fibreglass mattress, just the right material to provide cosy free accommodation for *Eliomys quercinus*, the animal the French call a *loir*. The place must have been full of the creatures. Their droppings were everywhere, on the floor, the shelves, the window-sills, the cooker, even in the sink and the loo. It may well have been sheer population pressure which sent some individuals to seek a home in other houses, causing a miniature migration like the lemming waves but on a smaller scale.

The first *loir* we saw at Soleil d'Oc ran across the rafters of the verandah while we were having breakfast. Soon, we saw more, and discovered their droppings deposited widespread over the kitchen during the night. I have always disliked the idea of poisoning or trapping animals that wished to share the hospitality of our home, but soon the *loirs* were becoming a real plague and nothing was safe from their sharp teeth. They would scrape holes in soft fabrics, seize upon any food incautiously left out, and then retreat to a haven under the dishwasher or behind the oven. They seemed to be everywhere, and in the end we had to resort to spring traps like conventional mousetraps but much larger, and these we would bait and set on shelves and on the rafters of the verandah. Generally, the *loirs* thought nothing of them and kicked them down to the floor during the night, when the sudden snap of the trap as it was sprung would wake us up. All the same, we killed a few – but always with sad hearts – and so were able to see these really very attractive creatures at close quarters.

The *loir* is no mouse. Six or eight inches long and with a fine bushy-tipped tail nearly as long again, it is half way to being a squirrel. The body is greyish brown and the face is golden in stripes, with a dark patch round the eyes. It is genuinely handsome and I always felt sad and guilty each time I removed the corpse of one more *loir* and reset a trap.

While we were absent in Jersey, the *loirs* had a celebration. High up in the living-room a porcelain cat which a friend had given us for our fiftieth anniversary was ensconced on a shelf, benignly grinning at whatever might be happening below. This was too much for the *loirs*. They scaled the cupboards up to its perch and pushed the cat over to smash upon the tiled floor. When we returned, the scattered fragments were there, thrown around the kitchen, as a challenge to us.

One November day, Jan and his foremen rollered the final coat of paint on the exterior walls of Les Cactus while we were glorying in the sensational autumn tints of the woodlands of the Montagne Noire. Two days later we raided a supermarket and filled the Volvo with empty cartons. Then we began to pack up.

Our grand-daughter was to be with us for a week to help with the packing. It fell to her to remove the extra bedding and curtains from the cupboards in the spare room where she slept, and she continually told us that she had heard somebody moving in her bedroom during the night. We pooh-poohed the idea, and assured her that there was obviously not so much as a *loir* in her room. It was not until she came to remove the final bath towel that a big *loir* shot out from beneath it, dived through her legs, swerved round Ingrid's feet and found sanctuary for a while under the sofa. Pursued, it disappeared through the surprisingly small space between the dishwasher and the wall, and was gone. But we never set the trap for it. After all, we were leaving, and the *loirs* could have the house to themselves. And if they could get in when they wanted, they could also leave the premises when they had finished up the crumbs.

We left Soleil d'Oc once more with everything packed up, and when we returned ten days before Christmas the moving began. It was the day of the rainbows too, for there were three brilliant ones during the morning, each set in a clear sky and spanning the village of Montouliers as we came round the red earth bend from Bize with a load of our belongings. It was an astonishing welcome, and we felt much as Noah and his family must have done when they saw the rainbow set in the sky as a sign of the unfailing care of Heaven. This extra touch of beauty seemed to radiate from the sky especially for our benefit, to tell us that we had found our real home.

The move lasted for three days, and always there was a rainbow to welcome us and to remind us ever to be grateful. Then came the night when, for the first time, we could sleep in this wonderful house we already loved so much.

Perhaps it was to bring me back to earth with a jolt that I suddenly fell out of bed.

5

Patience, But No Monument

As soon as we were properly in residence, I made a tour of the domaine with Étienne, and when we walked up the steps to where the hunting dogs had lived I pointed to the two sawn stumps on the side of the cliff and asked him who had cut down the two splendid *pin parasols*. His reply was decidedly non-committal; that is, he said – with a wave of his arm in a northerly direction – that it was the *patron*. I did not ask him who this alleged person might be, or what business he had in cutting down the trees and going off with the timber too, but when I said that we thought their removal was a blessing Étienne was very obviously relieved.

Étienne Clavel had been Madame Real's *gardien*. He actually did very little guarding, because he was only employed by her for one half day a week and his total armoury was a shovel, a pick-axe, a wheelbarrow, and the worn pair of wine-clippers. Along with the two dog kennels, he was almost all that was left over from the previous regime. Or I should say one dog kennel, for curiously enough the wooden one, about the size of a hen-house, had disappeared.

Étienne was the most brachycephalic individual I had ever met. His nearly bald head was an inch or two wider than it was high, and this meant that his smile was proportionately broader even if it was twisted by the need to keep one corner of his mouth clamped upon the treasured extinct end of a cigarette or small cigar – until, after a year or two, he suddenly gave up smoking from one day to the next, a fact which impressed us considerably even if we ourselves had done the same several years before.

At the outset, Étienne was something of a problem for us. He was around at the time of the sale and he had evidently liked Madame Real although he had a much greater admiration for her husband. He had worked at the house for some years, so to that extent he was part of the fittings. But his skills were unknown to us, and so was his character – just as we ourselves were unknown quantities to him. If we continued to employ him there was the risk that we might be exploited, or that it would always be a case of Madame Real did this, or Madame Real never did that. On the other hand, to sack him for no reason at all would be manifestly unjust, and it might also cause a bad smell in the village. We decided that the best course would probably be to negotiate more service than Madame Real had wanted from him, or had been able perhaps to afford, and then to see how things went on.

When I said to Étienne that we would like him to work more hours for us he was obviously pleased, but he at once gave the natural French answer that it was a matter which we should discuss with his wife. It was always the wife who ran the finances in France, from paying the bill after a restaurant dinner to negotiating any sales or purchases or hirings. It was she who held the purse-strings, and the husband was always to that extent her servant. We made a rendezvous with Madame Clavel, and at three o'clock in the afternoon – to allow the family three clear hours for lunch – we presented ourselves at the Clavel house on the corner opposite the post office.

It was the first time we had been in a house in the village.

The Clavel house had been one of the cafés in the days when Montouliers had enough inhabitants to make the trade of this institution and two other bistros worthwhile. There was a large parlour dominated by a gigantic television set but otherwise it was very sparsely furnished: a table, a chair or two, and not much besides. Several of the seven or eight grown-up children were there, chatting or smoking and paying no attention whatsoever to us. We sat down at the table as a committee of four, and I expressed the wish that Étienne could perhaps work three half days for us every week, provided, of course, that his various other jobs as a general factotum in the village and his work as a self-employed wine-grower in a small way would allow him to do so.

Étienne said nothing, but I could see he was pleased. Ingrid complimented Madame on the appearance of a tiny tot of a grandchild crawling under the table. Then we waited.

Madame said it could be arranged.

I then remarked that a certain sum had come into my mind, which in fact worked out at a round number of francs per hour. Madame considered, then indicated that a bargain could be struck along the lines I had suggested. Étienne beamed, but he did not interfere.

I took out my wallet and counted out the pay for the several half days which Étienne had already served. Étienne did not touch the notes, but Madame picked them up, counted them, and laid them on the table. The family paid no attention whatsoever and did not appear even to be listening to the conference.

Then there was a knock on the door. With a swift sweep of her hand Madame Clavel slid the money under the newspaper just as the mayor came in. She began to talk rapidly about the weather, and how cold it was or was not in the Anglo-Norman Isles, and whether the next winter might be better or worse. The mayor gave a message to Étienne in the half Catalan which I found so very hard to understand, and withdrew.

Madame Clavel drew out the notes again, counted them afresh and stuffed them in her purse. A glass of some not very expensive wine (three francs a litre), a handshake, and Étienne was informed that all was agreed.

Madame Real had made much of the excellence and value of a hideous fitting of shelves and cupboards with glazed doors

64

which extended across the whole of the rear wall of the living-room of Les Cactus. She had stressed that it was an antique, though anyone with cataract as well as myopia could see that it was built onto battens and had no back. It was probably a Lapeyre item, that being the firm which produced everything from doors and staircases to standard bedroom and living-room fitments of good design and finish. She wanted us to buy it, but we insisted that it would be a pity to take it from her. If she was so attached to it, should she not take it with her?

As soon as the house was ours I told Étienne he could have it, provided he could take it out and make good the wall.

During our next absence the fitting disappeared. But so did the wheelbarrow. I asked Étienne rather pointedly what he thought had become of it, and he said he thought the two lads working for Jan on the steps had stolen it. You never could tell with such lads, he said.

The heavy old-fashioned iron bath was now taken out of the bathroom by Jan, who was to replace everything with a proper modern suite from Anconetti's in Narbonne. The still service-able white loo was also removed. Both these items lay in the drive for some days before I asked Étienne if he would like them. He looked at the toilet bowl and said he thought one of his sons could do with it, and at the end of the morning he carried it away in his old Renault Quatre.

By now we had brought over the wheelbarrow from Soleil d'Oc, the one we had inherited from the Dutch widow. It was a standard French *brouette* the same as every other one might see, dark green and with a rubber-tyred wheel. One day, or maybe night, when we were away, it vanished.

I asked Étienne somewhat earnestly where he thought the barrow had gone.

'Ah, there are thieves everywhere. *Partout, partout. C'est incroyable,*' he said with a shrug.

Unbelievable. Very much so, and in spite of Madame's personal note to possible burglars I thought *incroyable* was literally correct. But I made no comment.

'Don't forget the bath, Étienne,' I said, as he left for lunch. Étienne came regularly at seven in the morning. The next day I was up before six and managed to lever the bath into our Volvo estate. Instead of driving through the village, I took the lane down past the spring at the bottom of the hill and drove to Bize, then over the river and on to Mailhac and almost to Pouzols to find the track which I knew led up the back of the Serre d'Oupia. A mile or more up this lane there was a deep *vallon* which served the village of Pouzols as a rather messy municipal dump or *poubelle*. I was familiar with this rubbish heap because I had passed it several times in Soleil d'Oc days when exploring the hills on foot.

I opened the back of the car and slid the bath out, but instead of tipping it into the ravine I left it at the side of the lane, for I was certain that it would quickly find a good home somewhere because baths were probably as scarce in Pouzols and Mailhac as they were in Montouliers. (In fact, by lunchtime the same day the bath had disappeared.)

Then I drove back to Montouliers, and put the car away. When Clavel arrived he looked around and could find no bath-tub anywhere. Surprised, he asked me what had become of it.

'There are thieves everywhere,' I said. 'Everywhere, Étienne. *Partout, partout.* You said so yourself, only yesterday,' I added with a smile.

Étienne did not know quite what to make of that.

'Look, Étienne,' I said. 'Madame and I have eyes here in the front of the head; we have them here also, on each side of the head, and we even have them in the backs of our heads. You understand that?'

Étienne understood very well indeed.

'You can pass that information on,' I said. 'Not, of course, that anyone around here would steal anything, *bien sur*. But just in case. Les Pilkingtons have six eyes, *compris*? Two in the front, two in the sides and two in the back.'

From that day forward we had service, and care, and mutual trust to a wonderful degree.

We brought our third wheelbarrow with us from Jersey. It was quite different in appearance from the French ones, and could never have been mistaken for another. And for some inexplicable reason the omnipresent thieves left it severely alone. Five years later it is still with us.

It was summer when we took possession, and not until late autumn that we lit our first log fire in the living-room on a pair of fire-dogs we had bought in Sallèles d'Aude to replace those which had disappeared with Madam Real. It lit well, with fir needles and pine twigs, and at once belched so formidably into the room that I thought we must have a nest in the chimney. But no, it was evidently clear right through, for a small amount of smoke – perhaps one tenth of the total, could be seen rising into the still, clear air. The remainder came billowing out to smoke us like mackerel.

'Must need sweeping,' I choked. 'Or perhaps once the draught is established the fire will begin to draw.'

We kept all the double doors open and piled on more sticks and pine-needles and logs. After a while the fire began indeed to draw, and soot came falling in lumps into the fire. Glowing lumps. I ran outside and saw three-foot flames spouting from the chimney pot and its side vents. I knew better than to put water on the fire and produce water-gas (one advantage of specializing in chemistry at an early age) but I brought the barrow in, loaded the burning logs and took them outside.

By now the chimney was something of a self-perpetuating blast furnace. Ingrid thought we should summon the pompiers, but I said No. By the time they were on the scene it would have burned itself out excellently, but I would myself go and look in the roof space to see that all was well amid the rafters.

It was. The brick of the chimney stack where it passed up toward the tiles was hot to the touch, but there were no cracks, nor any wooden structure passing into the brickwork. I saw it was safe to let the conflagration rip, and after another ten minutes we saw the flames abating, then dying right away. We now had a chimney thoroughly swept and clean, and no need to pay for a sweep.

So once again we lit the fire, and as the smoke had by now drifted out of the doors we closed them. The fire took well, then sent its smoke billowing out into the living-room just as before.

'Perhaps it's the wind,' Ingrid said.

'But there isn't any wind.'

'Well that could be a reason too.'

'There wasn't any wind when Madame Real had a blaze going,' I remembered.

'No. But we can't have this smoke. Better open the doors again.'

She did. And at once the fire drew perfectly. All the smoke went up the chimney in an eager and orderly fashion. I closed the doors and the room filled with smoke once more. I opened them and the fire drew again.

'Cunning of Madame,' I said. 'Don't you remember? She had the fire blazing, and said she wanted us to have the benefit of the sunshine too, so she had the doors wide open until we had left. And presumably until the fire went out too.'

Next day we called Jan, who was coming to finish the new double flight of steps from the terrace to the lawn, and we demonstrated our discovery. He was amused. Typically French, he thought. However, he knew that there was a man in Béziers who was an expert. He would fix it, Jan was sure. He had known him work miracles on flues, and the expert was self-confident enough to offer a no-cure-no-pay service. Jan would call him and invite him to come over.

Monsieur Bonnet arrived a few days later. He had a natty dispatch case, a suit appropriate to an insurance broker, and a tie – a rare enough object in the Minervois. He did not look as I expected a chimney expert to look, but he got on his knees to peer up the chimney, then went up the collapsible ladder into the roof space and even made an ascent of the tiles from outside to examine the top of the flue. Then he came down, dusted his knees and opened the executive case, which contained a flexible measure, a pad of blank paper, and another headed pad, on which to make estimates. He measured the chimney breast and took all the dimensions of the hearth.

'*Pas de problème,*' he said. And he made a little sketch. He would demolish the entire chimney breast and all the flue as high as the ceiling. He would rebuild it, but not in the same way. It had been constructed by cretins. But no problem. He would also place a new cap on the outside so that even the Tramontane and the Vent de la Mer could not blow the smoke down the chimney. The fire would be a delight, not an irritation. It was simple. He knew how to do it. He had rebuilt hundreds, maybe thousands of cretin-constructed flues. One had to have it in here (he tapped his head with his pencil).

Could he give an estimate?

Bien sur! He made some more measurements, and did some sums, then added 18.4% VAT with his calculator. He put it all neatly on an orange form and gave us a copy to sign. The total for this mighty work of reconstruction came to only three hundred and seventeen pounds.

'You agree? *Bon.* I may start on Tuesday?' M. Bonnet did not seem to suffer from the Occitan habit of thinking maybe-next-month-but-*ça-dépend*.'

We agreed. 'We shall expect your workmen . . .'

'*Non-non-non-non-non. C'est moi!*' And no cure, no pay.

Monsieur Bonnet was as good as his word. At eight o'clock on the Tuesday he was there again but had exchanged the natty suit for overalls. He covered the marble floor and the woodwork before attacking the chimney breast with a sledge-hammer. He was with us for three days, at the end of which the wall had been rebuilt and painted, the interior workings of the flue had been changed to his specification, and a neat new little hat sat on the exterior chimney. He cleaned up down to the last speck of dust, lit a fire, and admired the ascending smoke issuing from under the brim of the hat.

'*Voilà, monsieur et madame.*'

A cheque, a glass of wine, a vigorous handshake. '*Allez!*' and he was gone.

It was a few days later that a tall, lean man, head and shoulders higher than the other men we had seen in the village, came walking slowly up our entrance drive. We recognised him as the mayor. He was accompanied by a rather shrunken elderly woman with piercing spectacles and a squashed hat. The mayor informed us that she was Madame Cabanes.

We knew Madame Cabanes to be a remarkable woman. She was involved in various works of restoration in the *département* of Hérault and she lived in a fine and large house overlooking La Croisette, the crossroads in the village where all the gossip was exchanged while the women waited their turn at the travelling shop of the moment, which one day might be the butcher, another the *charcutier* from La Salvetat-sur-Agout, or perhaps the onion man who drove furiously through the village streets once a week with his hand on the horn of a car piled full of onions white and onions red.

Madame Cabanes had in fact saved the village. We were told this by herself, but also by others, and it was true enough. One morning several years earlier she had been startled by a grinding and clattering of machinery, and running out of her house had found a demolition gang about to start shovelling away the entire centre of Montouliers, which was ruined, collapsing and unsaleable. She told them to stop, hurried to tell the mayor that this frightful desecration must not be allowed, and then offered to buy the whole crumbling area herself. A mere hundred francs – and no doubt a lot of paperwork by a *notaire* – and it was hers. Thereupon she set about restoring the area, and the charming little alley now existing at the back of her house was the result, with everything done in excellent (and correct) style and with perfect craftsmanship.

And here she was, accompanied by the mayor, her eyes sweeping our domaine and noting every detail. The mayor opened the innings. What were we intending to do with the cave, he asked with barely concealed suspicion.

This cave was in the cliff which sheltered the house from the worst of the Tramontane. The opening was broad, but the cavity only went back for some twenty feet, although the back wall contained one or two holes which were large enough for a child to wriggle into, and maybe become stuck there. It figured on the picture postcards sold in the *épicerie*, and it was known once to have been inhabited.

I told the mayor that we were not intending to do anything with the cave beyond cleaning it up. Madame Real had used it as an incinerator, I pointed out, and the roof was sooty.

The mayor seemed relieved. 'The entrance to the cave belongs to the State,' he said. 'It is *classé.*'

'And the interior?'

'Maybe it is yours. Maybe not. It could belong to the land overhead.'

'And that is whose?'

'It is not easy to know.' The mayor went on to say that if the cave showed signs of collapsing, it would be the business of the *Mairie* to have workmen come and shore up the cliff and repair it. But that was impossible without coming on to our domaine, and indeed walking over our terrace.

'*Bien sur,*' I said. '*Pas de problème.*' I would write out a note authorising the mayor's workforce to walk freely over our property in order to deal with *dégâts* concerning the Grotte de Montouliers, and I would bring this document personally to the *Mairie* that same afternoon.

Madame Cabanes nodded, and the mayor was evidently satisfied with the reasonable attitude of these unknown newcomers to the village, one of whom at least was known to have his origin in a land renowned for perfidy, trickery and obstinacy.

'And the plantation? You will not be changing that?'

'*Non-non-non-non-non.*' We were tree lovers. We had the greatest admiration for the trees, I assured him.

'Planted by Monsieur Real, twenty years ago,' said Madame Cabanes.

'And very well done,' I put in. 'Only I intended to remove that dead poplar.'

'Of course.' The mayor nodded.

'And all the diseased elms. They are dying.' There were about thirty all told, most of them quite small, and I had brought a three-ton winch with us to haul them out by the roots. When I said so, I could see that the mayor was impressed.

'The trees are beautiful,' purred Ingrid. 'I have never seen such a fine collection.' Which was certainly true.

So the cave was safe, and the trees too. The mayor could breathe again. Madame Cabanes' eyes swept over the house and its new shutters which replaced the slit and shoddy ones of the Real era. She nodded appreciatively.

'Who made the shutters?'

'Monsieur Auziale at Capestang.'

'Ah. An excellent craftsman. Yes indeed. He has done work for me on some of my antiques.'

She observed the terrace and the new steps leading down to the lawn. Then she turned and looked at the roof.

'That chimney-pot is wrong. It is not in the style of the Languedoc.'

'Perhaps not,' I said.

'It should be exactly like the other.' Madame Cabanes pointed at the dummy one above the sun-room. 'They should be symmetrical.'

'That one is not a real chimney . . .'

'I am aware of that. But it is correct.'

I saw the mayor was smiling.

'You should change this one,' Madame Cabanes pursued. She said it with such authority that I realised the moment had come to put down the Pilkington foot gently, but quite firmly.

'We have changed the chimney because with the other one the house was filled with smoke,' I said. 'This one has been specially designed and tested as suitable by Monsieur Bonnet. He is a chimney expert from Béziers.'

71

'Ah. But it is not correct. It must be changed.'

'We need a fire,' I said as gently as I could, 'and with this chimney it is possible.'

'I do not think there is any need to change the chimney,' the mayor said quietly, with a reassuring look toward me. 'If it works, that is the main thing.'

'Exactly,' I agreed.

'Hm.' Madame Cabanes was not convinced, but with the mayor being so unexpectedly accommodating to these new-comers there was no more to be said.

Soon our visitors took their leave. I felt we had passed our first examination, if not with an alpha at least with a beta plus.

The Real Consorts Property

6

Noel, Noel

Our first Christmas at Montouliers was one of many surprises, most of them having little if anything to do with Christmas itself. On 20th December we had moved our final loads from Soleil d'Oc and bade farewell to the little house which had given us such a happy introduction to an area which, for ourselves, had no competitor anywhere. Then, in the evening, we turned on the illuminations.

As yet, we knew hardly anyone in the village of one hundred and eighty-six inhabitants. There was Madame Cabanes, and the mayor, his secretary, and, of course, Étienne and Madame Clavel. Otherwise, there were none that we knew by name, and our contact with them consisted in exchanging smiles and a handshake in the *épicerie*, the only shop in a village which once had had its own bakery too. The Jersey numberplate on our car was obviously a matter of curiosity, but I doubt if anyone could have said for sure whether the island was in Europe or America.

Montouliers being a humble, unpretentious village, with very meagre finances, there was not so much as a single string of lights across the village street at Christmas, so that was why we had to get busy with the illuminations. Our Christmas tree could soon be seen far and wide. When I wrote in a letter to a lady in Oxford, a heart and soul supporter of Oxfam, that we had decorated our thirty-foot Christmas tree with lights, I had an angry letter back. It was disgusting, she wrote, that we could think of buying a thirty-foot Christmas tree when half the world in Africa was starving. But we had not, in fact, written anything about buying a tree. It was there already, solidly planted at the edge of our lawn, and during the twenty years of its life had reached a handsome height.

The decoration, already used in earlier years on *faute de mieux* mimosas in Jersey and later on a pair of sadly scorched cypresses at Soleil d'Oc, consisted of long strings of those tiny lights which so tastefully adorn Christmas trees in Sweden and, in recent years, have even appeared in Oxford Street.

At first our tree was an innovation. Then it became a regularly accepted and indeed expected part of village Christmas. Within a year or two we had not returned to the village more than ten minutes before we were asked when we were going to put up the lights.

Today?

Yes, today, I said. As soon as I had brought them down from the attic. And I promised to get busy at once.

On Christmas Day we could see the snow glinting on the higher tops of the Cevennes to the north, and on our way to church at Narbonne we had a fine and clear view of the Pyrenees glistening white and formidable to the south-west. They looked inviting, but December was hardly the time to visit them except for winter sports. And we were too old for that. I had not been on skis (albeit in a decidedly amateur fashion), for thirty years and Ingrid (although much more expertly, as befitted someone from Sweden) for twenty.

For several years we had much preferred to celebrate Christmas in France than in Jersey, and probably two factors

74

were involved: the changing face of Christmas in the Anglo-Saxon world, and, of course, the fact that we were getting older, and with increasing age Christmas itself meant something different to us. Any family is likely to start with all the fun of a children's Christmas, with Santa Claus and stockings hung over the bed, and eventually this gives way to a rather heartier Christmas with plum pudding and turkey, and stacks of presents. Later, when the family is grown up or flown away, there is the socialising Christmas, with cocktail parties and the like, something which we ourselves had never found particularly to our taste. At the same time, the other side of Christmas had always been very real to us, and I don't think we would ever have wished to have the festival without feeling deeply its religious aspect.

Jersey reflected to a great extent the English pattern in which a gimlet-eyed female would remind one on the television at the beginning of October that there were only seventy-nine shopping days left before Christmas. Decorations appeared in the shop windows in London and Jersey also by mid-October, and a breathless rush of salesmanship would begin. Christmas in Anglo-Saxondom had gradually degenerated into little more than a super-commercial beano.

France was different, if only in a negative way. Christmas was barely observed at all. High pressure salesmanship was not a feature, Christmas trees appeared only during advent if at all, and the land was not flooded with gin – if only because people drank wine. The villages might have simple designs of coloured lights strung across the main street, but nothing more. Noel (fortunately the French word could not easily be debased, as in the English 'Xmas') was not commercialised, and for that matter it was not a notably religious festival either. Here and there a church might run to a watch-night service, but Christmas Day dawned like any other. The baker would bake, the grocer would groce, and in Narbonne the market would be in full swing until midday, just as it was on every other day of the year. And it was this very ordinariness of Christmas Day that appealed to us so much. The afternoon might see us walking over the hills, or perhaps we could relax in the sun. Most important of all, we could breathe the fresh air of all the love and goodness around us and think back to the Bethlehem of not so long ago and realise with special intensity the bravery of God entering village life as an artisan and going to certain death for showing people what he was really like, and how they should live their lives.

On Christmas morning we would go to Narbonne market, just as we did on Sundays. It was particularly well placed, being only a few minutes away from our church. This church referred to itself as a 'temple', a very clear indication of how deeply the hatred of the years of the wars of religion had bitten into the fabric of French life. Not that that hatred existed any longer, for Catholic and Protestant consistories nowadays worked perfectly well together, but it had been there in the past, and to such an extent that it was not until 1906 that the people of Narbonne were allowed to have a Protestant church (or temple) at all. There had been one earlier, but it had been destroyed during the wars of religion in the 1600s as part of the horse-trading between Colbert and the Catholics over the provision by them of money to complete the Canal du Midi.

Narbonne's temple was part of the Église Réformée de France, a sort of umbrella organisation and title which covers all non-Catholic and non-Orthodox churches except the 'way-out' ones. And of course it had a service on Christmas Day, to which we usually went, but the inherited mistrust of popery went so far as to embrace the decorations, which were austere to a degree. Earlier in the week there was a Christmas tree for the benefit of the children, but it was evidently considered too frivolous to be left in the church (or temple) over the *fête* of Christ's 'official' birthday.

We found this kind of purity rather annoying, so one year at the beginning of Christmas week I raised the subject with our cheerful Pastor Muller. I said I hoped he would leave the Christmas tree for us all to enjoy.

Pastor Muller was surprised at this suggestion, and he said it was not the custom. Why should the tree be there?

'Why not?' I said.

He smiled. 'It is not really anything to do with Christmas.'

'No. But what about that bit in Isaiah about the fir-tree and the pine coming to beautify the place of the sanctuary?'

He laughed – and the Christmas tree was allowed to stay in the church over Christmastide.

Just before New Year there was a sudden knock on the door. It was the holy hour of lunch and *digestif*, so I realised it must be something important. Monsieur Julien did not beat about the bush but introduced himself briefly as the owner of the vineyard on the other side of the lane. Did we wish to buy it? Or not?

Still at the cheese course I asked Monsieur Julien if he would give us a little time to consider. He said he would, and no doubt I would come down to his house by the bridge over the village stream and give him the answer later that afternoon. Then he nodded, put on his hat again, and left.

Now this matter of the vineyard was a very important one. The southern side of our property was bounded by a *chemin rural* which sloped down from near the church to the Fontaine de Bize at the bottom of the hill, and then doubled back up again to the main road beyond the *vallon*. In the crook of the *chemin* and reaching right along to the village was Monsieur Julien's long-established vineyard, edged by a number of large olive trees heavily laden with black fruit. They bordered the brambly ravine which went by the name of the *ruisseau du village*, though any water there might be was no more than a trickle hidden away in an impassable chasm of thorns. Across the stream was a melon-field, and beyond that a jumble of vineyard plots and a scatter of modern houses built by villagers who for one reason or another wanted to be free of the restrictions of the rather primitive houses in the village. Even before we were in possession of Les Cactus I realized that the Julien vineyard was as wonderful a building site as could be found in perhaps the whole of the Languedoc. It faced due south, the ground sloped away in front, the land basked in the sunlight and the view extended twenty miles to Narbonne cathedral and the cape at La Clape. It was a situation which, if skilfully developed, would almost rival our own.

We had no wish to build any houses. What was important was to prevent this vineyard falling into the hands of some English developer and having several houses erected straight in front of us. Admittedly, we would probably see over their roofs, but the lane would become a highway for at least the traffic involved in a handful of houses, and our peace and privacy would be very much affected. That was why we had earlier asked M. le Grix to enquire of M. Julien if he would sell his vineyard. And here was the answer. He would.

M. Julien was the only man in Montouliers except for André Fraisse, the mayor, and myself, who was so much taller than the general run of villagers that he could at once be seen protruding above any gossiping group of men. In fact, he was aloof from most of the village activities, but he was reputed to be a clever businessman and, of course, he knew very well that our apparent interest in the vineyard had nothing to do with a desire to make a ton or two of red plonk. When he arrived during the lunch hour he had given us a figure at which he would sell, a figure which was very much larger than the value of a vineyard with about eight hundred bearing vines of carignan and aramon.

Ingrid and I discussed it, and we also phoned M. le Grix. He confirmed our suspicion that M. Julien would not be beaten down in price. If we declined, he would probably sell the land as a number of building plots.

Of course he might not at once succeed, but the sale of even one plot straight in front of us would be a serious blow to ourselves and would certainly destroy the glorious peace of the whole environment. We were safely protected on all other points of the compass, because the land either belonged to us or was vineyard or cliff or pinewood, but the southern aspect was very definitely vulnerable. M. Julien would be well aware of this, and with the encouragement being offered by the EEC to reduce the vineyard area of the Languedoc he would have no trouble at all in getting building permission for several houses.

'Buy it,' said M. le Grix. 'Keep all the area in front of you and then sell the remainder for building. You can probably get your money back. *Pas de problème.*'

It did not take us long to decide. I walked down through the vineyard and told M. Julien that it was a deal. We would sign the agreement on the following day.

Next morning, Ingrid and I walked down the lane and up toward the main road that led to the Juliens', the house right by the bridge over the village stream or ditch. Le Grix was waiting for us. The house was only the second one in the village that we had been inside, and, like others that we came to know later, it was almost as dark as night even on the brightest of mornings. It seemed to be the custom in our village (and in others, too) to shut the shutters at night so that not a crack of the precious electric light could escape into the ambient air. The shutters were usually kept tight shut during the day also, either to avoid the work of closing them at nightfall or to keep out the warmth, or to provide a milieu for viewing the non-stop flow of rubbish poured out by six television channels, or to keep insects from relieving themselves on the glass, or to frustrate prying eyes, or to preserve the colour of the indoor fabrics, or maybe just because grandma had always done it that way.

The Juliens differed a little from the others in that they actually partially folded back the shutters of one or two of the windows on the ground floor which were shaded by mulberry trees neatly pruned and trained. But it was still dark enough in the house for the electric light to be on in the passage behind the front door, and M. Julien immediately turned on a lamp when he led us into the parlour, even though outside the winter sun was shining brightly. The room was presentable and could even have been reckoned a pleasant one if it had not been decked out in the familiar kind of gloomy and unsightly wallpaper so favoured by the French eye, and furnished with the usual bleak French furniture. We ranged ourselves round the table, and Madame Julien came in and sat nervously at the end. For once it was not the lady of the house who conducted the business, but she had to be there to sign.

Le Grix had all the papers. There was the familiar *lu et approuvé* and *bon pour achat* to be written in our own handwriting, and a cheque was passed. At a sign from her husband, Madame Julien went to the cupboard for a bottle of their own *muscat* and five glasses. We drank, shook hands, and the vineyard would – after the familiar notarial time-lag – be ours.

This time-lag worried me. After all, we were buying a vineyard, and it was time to set about pruning. All across the landscape one could see solitary muffled figures bent over the vines, snipping at the unwanted shoots of the previous season. We could hardly expect Monsieur Julien to carry on with the maintenance of the vines if he were not to see the results of his labours, but if we ourselves waited for the passing of the *acte* we would lose the crop of the coming year. And it was usually considered risky to start work of any kind on a property that was not one's own, whether a contract was duly signed or not. So before signing I raised this point. If Monsieur Julien could not go back on the deal I could see no danger in asking for permission to work the vines, and le Grix said it made sense. The Juliens readily agreed – maybe they had wondered if they would be expected to keep the vineyard in order during the period of paper gestation.

We knew how much of the land we had bought. The area was already agreed and clearly set out on the village plan at the *Mairie*. Our boundaries were the lane, a high bank, the village stream, and on the Julien side a path, a yard or two broad, beyond which was the small patch of vines which he had wished to retain.

'To make *muscat* for my own use,' he explained. His *muscat* was extremely good, as we discovered when we tasted it. 'It's not much – maybe a hundred litres, just enough for ourselves.'

Monsieur Julien was going to make sure there were no ambiguities, no risks of encroachments by the Pilks. He had arranged for a couple of surveyors to measure the exact position of the path boundary and insert into the ground some kind of holy official mark which could never be removed without fearful penalties. I said that was a sound idea, but he could pay the bill. And I added that I would attend in person when the surveyors were there. I wanted to be sure they had their instructions correctly.

The boundary ceremony took place a week later. Two pleasant individuals dressed in such a way as to emphasise that they were professional experts and not mere yokels, made a great show of calculating the metric equivalents of rods, poles and perches. They triangulated and hypotenused and theodolited with as much energy as if they were the two men sent out by Louis XVI to decide the length of the metre by triangulating the whole distance from Dunkirk to Barcelona. They squinted through instruments, unreeled tape measures of impressive length, worked out angles, put sticks in the ground, did sums, and measured the distance from an olive tree to a bramble root. They established the corner point, which curiously enough turned out to be just where I had marked it with my heel. A hole was dug, cement was poured into it, a metal mark was set in it, and no doubt suitable curses were muttered to fall upon the head of any Pilk or other wicked creature who might dare to alter the boundary. The frontier was now officially demarcated.

As we walked home through the vines which would soon be ours, but which we might even now work, Ingrid stopped.

'You know what has happened . . .' she began.

'Happened?'

'Yes. With the signing of the contract we have become something neither of us had really dreamed of. We are now *vignerons*!'

Which was true. And with the harvest we should be *viticulteurs récoltants*. Because we certainly had no intention of letting the vineyard go to ruin, and not just because we knew that an untended vineyard was a paradise for every conceivable kind of pest from rabbits to oidium and mildew, and that one could be held liable to *procés verbal* if the plagues spread, as they most certainly would, to the neighbouring vineyards. No. All good things around us were sent from heaven above – and that included some eight hundred stocks of *carignan* and *aramon*, the very stuff that plonk was made of.

It was one thing to decide that we were going to keep the vines and run the vineyard as respectable and responsible members of a community where there was no other trade or occupation than that of vintners, but we now had seriously to set about an occupation in which we had no experience. Ingrid was an expert in blood analysis, I, in off moments, had been a reasonably accomplished lobster-potter. But *vignerons*, even on a small scale, was something very different. It was now the end of the year, the vines were dormant and the dead leaves were sweeping through the rows of bare stocks on the crest of a wave of Tramontane. Where were we to begin?

Ingrid thought we should telephone the Bonnels and ask their opinion of our purchase. The necessary care of any immediate work could safely be entrusted to Clavel. We rang Christian at his home at Aigne, and he drove over at once.

Christian Bonnel was our earliest Minervois friend, and we had known him even before our Soleil d'Oc venture. It happened that in a village restaurant somewhere in the area we had had a bottle of wine with our dinner, a wine which we thought was sufficiently good for us to load a quantity of it

aboard and transfer it to our Volvo en route for Jersey when we
laid up *Thames Commodore* for the winter at Aigues Mortes.
Having noted the Bonnel phone number from the wine label, I
rang. Could Monsieur Bonnel bring four cases of red Domaine
de la Lecugne and two of white down to the boat? We were
about ten miles away, lying against the bank under the trees,
on the Argeliers loop, not far from the Pont d'Argeliers. *Bien
sur*, he could, and that afternoon a Mercedes came bumping
along the tow-path to deliver the wine at our gang-plank.

Christian was a stocky man, bursting with energy as well as
competence. At the moment he was wearing a rather German-
style cap, which did not improve his appearance, but we found
him warm, enterprising and exuberant. When now, a few years
later, he answered our summons and came to survey our new
acquisition from the lane above, he told us that several years
earlier, before he bought a house at Aigne, he had been
stationed on the road to Bize on the further side of the *vallon* as a
steward during one of the cycle races in the area. The course
turned a somewhat blind bend where the road led out of
Montouliers, and his duty had been to warn approaching
traffic of cyclists hurrying toward the corner unable to see
ahead. Whilst waiting for competitors, he had several times
turned round and looked with admiration and longing upon
the house nestling among the beautiful cypresses and pines on
the other side of the stream and vineyard. It was, he said, the
only house he had ever really wanted to own; but it was not
then for sale.

'*Mon cher* Roger, *chère chère* Ingrid. Congratulations. It is a
house in a million. And that it is you who have bought it – that
is my greatest happiness!'

We walked out to the lane and Christian's gaze swept over
our new acquisition.

'*Impeccable!*' This would be the best siting for houses in all the
area, he said. Far superior to the plots the *Mairie* was trying to sell,
and which none of the locals could be persuaded to buy because
they had reservations about having the cemetery as their only
neighbour. Yes, it was excellent. Why, one there, another down
there, maybe four altogether; yes, why not sell the top half as far
down the lane as the hawthorn, and keep the rest? Sell two sites,
each for half what we had paid for the whole vineyard, and then –
pftt! It would be done and a good bargain too.

I said we thought not. We certainly could sell off half, but then we would have traffic, and perhaps worse, and no longer the full beauty we had now. I pointed across to the side of the Pech, where a new house was left unfinished, and a collection of broken-down and useless vehicles was scattered over the terrain.

'It could become like that,' I said.

Christian nodded. 'It is true. There are many pigs in France.' He considered. 'Of course, you could pull out the vines and put in a peach orchard. Peaches would do well there.'

That was true. There were some fine orchards of peach and nectarine and apricot in the region, and especially down in the plain of the Aude. But I saw a difficulty. If we grew a ton or two of peaches they would need not only to be picked but to be marketed. There was not enough traffic passing through the village for us to sell off that quantity of fruit merely by putting it for sale on the wall as farmers did with their vegetable crops in Jersey. The advantage of vines was that one had only to pick the grapes and the wine co-operative did the rest. Ingrid and I had decided to keep the whole vineyard and work it, I said.

'*Bon!* So you wish to be *vignerons*, like me!' Christian exclaimed. 'Then let me tell you what you can do.'

Christian pointed out that coping with the ordinary form of vine, growing out in all directions as a bush, could be back-breaking when it came to harvesting. However, one could stretch vines along wires, held by intermediate metal stakes, and then train the vines espalier-fashion so that they expanded in two dimensions instead of three. But a quick calculation in my head told me that this was out of the question. It would be an enormously costly operation, and the vines were not worth it. In a newly planted vineyard it might perhaps be sensible, but not in this case where some of the vines were already geriatric.

No, we would carry on with the vineyard, the whole of it, just as it was before. We would prune, and Étienne Clavel could add his expertise with dusting and spraying and fertilising. One day, nine or ten months later, we would have our reward of handling the big bunches of blue-sheened grapes from our very own vineyard. Yes, we were *viticulteurs*, and proud of it. I could almost smell the heady odour of juicy, red, fermenting wine.

But that hypothetical aroma was still a long way off, and meanwhile we had other matters to occupy us. Such as changing our small car.

Our first little car in France was bought from the Renault agent in Lézignan. The purchase was simple enough. Sign the contract, wait three weeks for the phone call to say it had arrived, and contrive to reach Lézignan to take delivery. I was then advised to drive to the licensing authority at the other side of the town to acquire the '*carte grise*' which would give us a registration number. With this we could then go to the insurance office and have the car insured.

Nothing could be simpler, except that I refused. Nothing would induce me to drive an unlicensed and uninsured car through a French town, I said.

Then we could not have the car. *Voilà.*

'Nor you the cash. Give me the contract and I will tear it up,' I said, trying to smile pleasantly. I had not yet handed over the cheque.

So, of course, one of the mechanics was told to drive this typically awkward Anglais to the tax office. The car was licensed and insured in a matter of minutes and we all parted good friends.

Our little Renault had plenty of use, as we always liked to have a small car to lend to the friends and relatives who came to stay, from Soleil d'Oc days onwards. And now the time had come when we thought we would trade it in and buy a new one. Again, nothing could be simpler, surely. And as we had in Bize a small Renault garage, run by an even smaller but very efficient Monsieur Soler, I thought it would be pleasant to support local industry and allow the order to pass through his hands. He would have no trouble in placing the order through the area distributor, which was the garage at Lézignan, and he could collect the commission on the sale. I signed the contract, waited three weeks, and then Monsieur Soler phoned to say that I was to go to Lézignan to sign the papers.

'*Non.*'

'*Non?*'

'*Non.* They can put them in the post, to you.'

That seemed to raise difficulties, but after much negotiation it was agreed that the papers would be brought over to Bize by the van which delivered spare parts. Next day M. Soler phoned to say the papers were there, in Bize. Would I collect them?

'Of course.'

The papers were not, as I expected, an application for a *carte grise*. They were only the first move in the game of grandmother's steps which led in that direction, and consisted of a document to be signed and stamped at the *Mairie* to certify that our address was correct.

Monsieur Fraisse, having been mayor for more than forty years, was thoroughly used to demands of this nature and after a brief talk about the outlook for the *vendanges* he signed the form and Claudette neatly imprinted the rubber stamp of municipal authority. Then I returned to Bize.

Monsieur Soler telephoned the distributors to say that he had the paper, properly signed and stamped, and would send it back with the spare parts man. Then they could get the *carte grise*, and the Renault would be delivered. Nothing could be simpler.

Next morning he phoned and asked me to go over to Bize for the final arrangements. He had, I assumed, the *carte grise* and the number plates. But no, he had the paper back which I had handed to him the previous day, and I was to take it to the prefecture at Montpellier.

'Montpellier? That is ninety kilometres away.'

'But if you take the motorway you would be there in two hours,' said Monsieur Soler gently.

'I'm not going to Montpellier,' I said. 'The distributors can go if they wish, but not me.'

M. Soler was sad, but he sympathised. He phoned Lézignan and said that Monsieur Pilkington did not wish to go to Montpellier. Perhaps they could arrange it. A long conversation ensued, at the end of which he put down the phone and said he was desolate, but they said I must go to Montpellier myself. That was where the prefecture was, and that was that.

'I am not going,' I said. 'What, drive all that way there and back taking more than half the day to get a piece of paper? Certainly not.'

'You mean . . . No?' He looked as though he were going to cry.

'Certainly. I refuse to go to Montpellier. *Pas de discussion*. I am not going.'

'Then perhaps there will be difficulties, and the car cannot be delivered,' he said sadly.

'*Tant pis*,' I said. 'But I refuse. I shall not, not, not go to Montpellier.'

There followed another long discussion with Lézignan, then M. Soler approached me with his hand over the mouthpiece.

'I have an idea,' he said, with the appealing look of a spaniel who hopes he will be allowed to lick the plate. 'There is a sub-prefecture in Béziers. Would you be willing to go to Béziers?'

I looked at Ingrid, who nodded. We liked M. Soler and he was definitely on our side in these negotiations. Besides, it would be sad if the cup of commission were to be snatched from his lips through failure of the sale to materialise. I said yes, in a spirit of compromise I would go to Béziers, provided that everything I had to take to the office there was to hand. Greatly relieved, M. Soler passed on the news that we were ready to oblige, and Lézignan agreed that anything necessary would be in Bize with the spare parts delivery next morning by eight o'clock. So everyone was happy, and even if I did not altogether accept the necessity of the journey to Béziers, I was prepared to do it.

On the following morning we set off in good time with the papers, the chassis number and a lot more erudite information, a map of Béziers on which our destination was marked, and a driving licence from the Paroisse de St. Brelade in Jersey. I also took our passports, a cheque book, the insurance cover-note of our Volvo which extended cover to any car we happened to want to drive, and a Jersey bus pass with which I thought I could confuse officials if necessary. We arrived at the sub-prefecture at ten twenty-five – which was fortunate, as at ten thirty they closed for lunch and a notice informed a rather hostile collection of *carte grise*-seekers outside the bars of the gates that the office would re-open at three.

Within a few minutes the papers were processed and a girl brought them to the *guichet* window. She was just handing them over when she hesitated, and drew them back.

I was not domiciled in France, she said pleasantly. But I had given a French address. Unfortunately, it would not be possible to issue the *carte grise* without my producing a certificate from the prefecture in Montpellier giving us permission to reside in the *département*. Sorry, but – and she looked at her watch – they were closing now. Maybe I would return another day . . .

Behind the *guichets* there were several licensing clerks dealing with other customers, and to the right a *chef de bureau*, tired and harassed looking, in shirt sleeves. I raised my voice almost to a shout, not in the anger which I tried to conceal but so that everyone in the office could hear.

'I thought every office in the whole of France knew that a certificate of residence is not required by citizens of the E.E.C. countries,' I declared, very loud and very clear. 'Everyone knows that. Is that not so?'

The girl hesitated, and glanced to her right and left. She received non-committal glances of sympathy from her neighbours.

I repeated it. 'Everyone knows that. Citizens of the E.E.C. . . .'

Hearing something like an incipient riot or commotion, the *chef de bureau* emerged from his office clutching a bundle of files.

'If you are in doubt, ask the *chef*,' I said in a mollifying voice. 'He will confirm it. He will certainly know' – and I pulled out the stops again – 'as everyone knows, that a E.E.C. national has the right as decreed by the Council of Europe to reside in any country of the E.E.C. that he chooses.'

All eyes were now on the *chef de bureau*. The girl repeated my statement in case he had not heard it already. 'Is that the case?'

He hesitated for a moment. I could see that the 'everyone knows' had scored a direct hit. What would the *homme-plus-grande-que-moi* have to say if he went against an E.E.C. directive, or even admitted ignorance of it.

'*Mais oui!* The monsieur is quite correct,' he said. '*C'est bon.*' And he returned to his desk.

The girl passed the papers to me with a pleasant smile. 'And now you can obtain the *vignette*,' she said. That, I knew, was the adhesive licence disc.

'But I thought . . .'

'*Non-non-non-non-non.* This paper gives the number, but not the *vignette*. That will be issued if you take it to the tax office in the area where you live. Your garage will tell you.'

Monsieur Soler was mightily relieved when, after a suitable pause for the lunch hour or two or three, we returned to his garage at Bize and showed him the paper. The sale was almost complete now.

'And where is the tax office?'

He consulted his mechanic, and a man who was having the wheel changed on an old Deux Chevaux. Yes, that was it, of course. Sallèles d'Aude, *pas loin*.

I knew Sallèles, because it was on the branch canal which led to Narbonne and the sea. It was not more than a quarter of an hour away. The tax office, the mechanic thought correctly, was in a house on the right bank of the canal. I could not miss it.

That was also correct. I walked along the whole row, but there was no notice of an inspectorate, so seeing an elderly lady sitting at the unshuttered window of one of the houses, I knocked on the glass and asked her if she knew where the *percepteur* could be found.

But of course. She pointed up through the ceiling, and I went upstairs to an office with shelf upon shelf of files of tax returns. Two girls and the *percepteur* were there, working in the pallid glare of strip lights. They were delighted to help, and *monsieur le percepteur* was only too willing to chat about the sad decline in the traffic of tanker barges filling their tanks at the Castelvin wharf to take the wine to Bordeaux for blending. But it was a good year for peaches, he thought. And with luck the *vendanges* would be good this year provided the weather held, as it certainly would, he was sure.

The girl brought the *vignette* and he stamped it, then shook me by the hand. It was a pleasure to be of service.

I was half way to the top stair when he called me back. There was an unfortunate mistake. Yes, he had not been thinking. A thousand apologies, but the *vignette* was not valid.

'What??'

'No, no. Montouliers is in the Hérault. This is the Aude. Bize is in the Aude, so is Sallèles. But not Montouliers. No. And the *vignette* has to be issued in the correct department. Any tobacconist will do it late in November in the right department. At other times the tax office, *bien sur*, but only a tax office in the Hérault.'

And where, I asked, might that be?

The staff consulted. Could it be Béziers? Yes. No. Maybe. Perhaps not. Surely there was one closer.

'Quarante?'

They could not say. They were charming, all three, and very anxious to help. 'But you understand, Monsieur, that we know very little of the Hérault.' Curiously there came into my mind the words of Neville Chamberlain in 1938. 'Czechoslovakia is a country of which we know very little.' It was as though I were wanting information about a country in Central Africa. They advised me to try Capestang.

Just ahead of closing time I found the tax office. There was no indication on the outside of the house, but there were two ladies in an office inside the courtyard of what must once have been a vintner's premises. They took the money, issued the *vignette*, and we had completed a good day's work. Our new car could now be fetched from Lézignan. That I left to M. Soler, who drove over with the returning spare parts man on the following day.

7

The Chevalier

When we had completed our move to Montouliers we were the proud possessors of two houses: Les Cactus and Number Twenty, Soleil d'Oc. This, of course, was one more than we wanted, and our first property had to be put up for sale. By this time we had been in several of the Dutch houses, because Hollanders who were tired of the area, or of the outlook over the cinder fields, had a way of asking us in to look their place over, just in case we knew somebody who would want to buy it. There seemed to be a widespread idea that the British were the most likely customers because they were stupid and would have no idea of values. The only reason why some of the Dutch were still there, year after year, was the ridiculous price of over half a million francs that they had put on their properties. I advised them to accept a lower offer if one should be made, but they said *Nei!* Six hundred thousand was what their house was worth.

These little, badly designed and poorly constructed houses often remained unsold for a very long time. Nobody seemed anxious to buy a shoddy building with primitive and restricted plumbing for the price of a decent house. Number Twenty was a much better bargain, because it had insulation, double-glazing, and two proper bathrooms and two toilets. And the price was not much above half what was being asked for other bungalows. After discussing it with le Grix we had put a figure on the property which was realistic and was about right, we thought, in terms of what we had spent on improvements.

After a while, le Grix telephoned to say that he had a buyer at this reasonable price. Monsieur Teisseyre was normally resident somewhere in the faraway Francophone Orient, where he conducted the business of his company in several different currencies, as each of his various areas of action had its own – to say nothing of a different language. The offer was an unexpectedly good one, and the *notaires* to be involved were our own friend Maître Salsa from Capestang and the Dutch widow's *notaire* for Monsieur Teisseyre.

We never met Monsieur Teisseyre until the day of the signing of the *acte* at the notairial office. He was a large man of about sixty, well turned out and with a curling moustache. He was wearing a black businessman's jacket and striped trousers, rather unusual clothing for mid-July in the Minervois, even if this particular day had so far only clocked up thirty-two degrees in the shade, but it gave him a very proper air of being a man of far-flung commercial interests. He was accompanied by madame, a very attractive black lady of about thirty, who was fluent in English and turned out to be a graduate in management of the University of Sussex. In chatting to this charming lady in the waiting-room I understood that Monsieur Teisseyre had selected that spot as a residence for her in France because he had carefully studied the charts of rainfall and sunshine and temperature, and had come to the conclusion that no other area of metropolitan France approximated so closely to the warm conditions of her own country in the distant French Caribbean.

We took our seats formally along one side of the table; Maître Salsa, Ingrid, Theisseyre, myself and madame from the Caribbean. Across the table was the home-pitch *notaire*. He produced the *acte* for us to *lire-et-approuver-et-bon-pour-vente* in our own handwriting, and I thought it wise actually to read through the main part of the *acte*. When I came to the sentence which mentioned the price I was surprised to see that the figure was fifty thousand francs too low, and I was just pushing the paper along the table to Salsa, pointing at the error with my finger, when I felt something on my knee which I took to be the chin of the *notaire's* Briard, a large kind of rather amiable sheepdog, with a woolly coat, stand-up and turn-over ears, and a notable lack of intelligence. I put my hand under the table to stroke the creature, but what I felt was not the nose and shaggy face and ears of a large dog, but a packet of paper. Feeling it, I could detect the rubber band around the leaves, and I realised at once from the nature of the paper and the size of the individual pieces that it was a sizeable bundle of banknotes.

91

Large enough, in fact, to account for the drop in price on the contract paper.

I understood. I nodded to Monsieur Theisseyre and smiled to his *notaire*, pulled back the paper of the *acte* and signed it as *bon pour vente*. Ingrid signed too, and so did Theisseyre. The proceedings were then over. I had noticed casually that madame had not signed, but I presumed that if the lawyers were evidently content, that did not matter.

In fact, I am not certain that the Theisseyres ever resided at Number Twenty, as I believe they intended to do, although they had a house-warming party the next day to which we were invited along with some of the Occers and also Wiesmann the plumber, whose legs protruded from beneath the kitchen sink while he was fixing some of the joints that had come apart during the frosts of winter. The lady of the house was quite charming, and we hoped to see her again.

But we never did. Perhaps the similarity to the climate of the Caribbean became less obvious when mid-winter arrived and even the Canal du Midi was frozen, as it was that year.

New Year dawned in sunshine, and from our bedroom window we saw a red squirrel run up the poplar in excitement. No hibernation for him, thank you very much, with the temperature on the first day of the year reaching 19° in the shade and 26° in the sun. He could be as active as we, though of course his small size meant that there were limits to what he could tolerate, for in such a small warm-blooded animal the ratio of surface (through which heat is lost) to the body to be kept warm was so much higher. A nice fur coat was a help, and if now our squirrel friend could keep himself warm enough to enjoy New Year's Day eating the juicy bits of cones on our huge umbrella pine, the time was soon coming when he would have to give up and revert to the cold-blooded habits of his distant ancestors, and stop almost all activity. For although a week of moderately warm sunny days lay ahead, the Great European Freeze was on the march from the north. A cold air-stream was spreading down the map.

By the tenth day of the year the thermometer in Leningrad had dropped to -55°, in Stockholm -26°, and in Montouliers +2°. But the cold increased as the polar air arrived. On the twelfth the midday temperature was only one degree above freezing, and for the next ten days the nights brought hard frosts. Puddles were iced over, the cold water pipes froze in the roof space, even the Canal du Midi was frozen hard enough to be walked upon. The great motorway to Spain was blocked by thirteen hundred lorries immobilized by the solidifying of their diesel fuel. Somewhere the squirrel was safely and soundly asleep.

We endeavoured to keep our regular after-lunch walks, but sometimes the Tramontane blowing at seventy miles an hour from the snow-clad and frozen mountains persuaded us to give up and sit by the fire instead. The small birds seemed to survive, but we lost all our geranium cuttings when Jan's builder lads took the covers off them to place over some fresh concrete.

In March, things were very different. A large green stick insect came to sit with us on the terrace seat. The village women began to emerge and sit in the spring sunshine. We had our sacred rite of tea out-of-doors, and supper could include a dish of wild asparagus from the domaine. On the last day of the month a 'V' of very large birds flew high overhead, heading north. We were evidently on the migration route which the storks took when flying from north Africa to their nesting sites in Alsace perhaps, or Holland and Denmark. And next day was when the first lizard peeped out to warm itself in the sun, and I myself changed to short trousers for the summer which was now making its impending presence felt.

A week later we had our first scorpion, sitting indoors behind the log basket. It was a black one, very much like a miniature lobster. These black scorpions were amiable creatures, and we became used to finding them lurking behind the shutters ready to grab a passing woodlouse or other creepy-crawly. They were charming little animals and yet we found that the sight of one could fill some of our visitors with almost hysterical fear, as though the harmless creature could slay them merely with a glance.

April was always an eventful month. There would be a village carnival at Bize or Sallèles-d'Aude or Ginestas with everyone out to celebrate the coming summer. It was the time for the frogs in the Cesse at Bize to shout their coarse love-songs from their positions on top of the thick water weed. The Scops owl would 'poop, poop' from an olive tree in our lower vineyard, and the big emerald lizards would appear. The wild

Judas trees were glowing venous-blood red in the hedges, the lilac was out, and some of the limestone scarps were bright with the wild Cheiranthus wallflower, and the *garrigue* with the deep violet short-stemmed *Iris chamaeris*. By now the vines were well in bud and the leaves breaking. And it was time for Étienne and myself to start the search for the colonies of the pine processionary (*Thoumetopoea pityocampa*).

The first time I saw the processionary was in Gibraltar. A long line of hairy caterpillars was marching in column, head to tail, their leader taking them purposefully, like the Grand Old Duke of York, to march to the top of the post and then down again. The next encounter was when Ingrid and I were out for a walk in Cyprus and we came upon what looked like a thin rope lying across the road from side to side. Except that it was clearly moving in a series of localised waves. We counted the caterpillars. There were one hundred and fifty-four in a marching column about twenty yards in length.

Breaking the orderly march by diverting one of the troop made no difference. They quickly joined up again. We found the procession interesting, the military precision of the members of the cohort rather endearing. But in those days we were not the owners of pine-trees and had no idea of the damage they could cause, wiping out whole woods at a time.

The moth would lay its eggs in quantity on the shoot of a pine-tree, and the baby caterpillars began at once to spin a protective silken tent around the whole family. These whitish encampments were about the size of an orange, or larger, and the caterpillars inside them would feed on the bark of the pine until they had exhausted the supply. Then one of them, chosen I know not how, would decide it was time to leave and would lead the whole lot like a Pied Piper, abandoning the tent as they descended in procession down to the ground.

As for the tree, nothing could save the branch where they had pitched their tent, and I suspect this was because of something in the excreta which acted as a virulent weed- or tree-killer, for it is well known that if the prickly hairs are extracted with ether they cause no irritation to the skin, whereas the excreta do.

A year or two later we were walking on the hills near Cébazan and came to a plantation of young Corsican pines heavily infested, with some of the trees already dying. I thought the simplest way to deal with the situation was to close my fist round the shoot and pull the whole tent off over the tip. Already in the evening I knew I had made a mistake, but a good dose of anti-histamine with a pain-killer washed down with whisky put things right overnight.

It was not difficult to see the tents if they appeared on our trees. The problem was to get at them, but I bought an extra-long extensible pruner and Étienne would climb a tree or balance on a two-way ladder to reach the enemy. Up to twenty-five feet above the ground was within range, but beyond that it was a matter of climbing monkey-wise. Every spring we would find two or three nests, and the only possible fate for them was the bonfire. One day a couple of years later I was driving up the lane above the village and saw that an infestation had begun. I ran back for my gloves and the pole-clipper and a couple of plastic sacks and managed to cut off one hundred and eight affected shoots, which had then all to be consigned to the fire. If somebody, in this case myself, had not acted promptly the entire woodland would have been lost. I never liked burning even caterpillars alive as though they were so many Joan of Arcs, but if it was a case of choosing between the processionaries and the pines, the trees had my vote every time. And the next year I removed two hundred colonies.

Apart from being a self-appointed exterminator of parasitic larval lepidoptera, I had plenty to occupy me in April. And it was a very beautiful time of the year as the spring broke in the Minervois. It could be snowing in Paris, but with us the days were warm and in the second half of the month the tempera-tures would now and again break the 20° level. In the woodland where we often walked after lunch the Cleopatra butterfly was flying, a tiny golden narcissus was waving in the breeze, and the Styrax was in flower, a curious bush which is much used in Orthodox lands for incense, and the kernels of its fruit for making rosaries. The first hire-boats would be on the move along the canal, where the yellow water-irises would be lining the banks with gold. By mid-month the cuckoo had arrived, and the need to pay a property tax was imminent. This tax had to be paid by the middle of May, unrequested but accompanied by one's own assessment of value made on a particular form.

To obtain this form I tried the post office, the *sub-préfecture* in Béziers, the *trésor public* in Puisserguier and the *percepteur* in

95

Ginestas. None of them had heard of either the form or the tax, but the *percepteur* advised me to try our *Mairie*. Claudette, the secretary, was as puzzled as the others had been, but Monsieur Fraisse our faithful mayor of more than forty years standing had a sensible suggestion to make.

'If none of the tax offices have the form, why bother to pay the tax?'

A good idea, I thought, and a typically French one. And had we been natives we might very well have done nothing, just as he had suggested. But we were as yet comparative strangers in the land, and we were vulnerable. Besides, no less than three English settlers in the area had skipped the country leaving debts with village tradesmen, quite apart from unpaid bills with the public services and the taxman. One of our constant preoccupations was to try to damp down the very natural feeling – though not in our own village – that the British were invariably a set of scoundrels who were not to be trusted.

In the end it was Narbonne's immense Hôtel des Impôts which produced the form. But only with obvious unwilling- ness. 'Montouliers – that is in the Hérault,' said a rather fierce woman as she looked through the racks of papers. 'This is the Aude.'

'I know, but . . .'

'You should obtain the form in Béziers.'

'Of course, madame. Certainly. But I have my hair cut in Narbonne, and I thought it would save a journey.'

'But your own authorities are the ones to help you,' she said, pushing the forms through the window. 'However, this time we will oblige.'

I made suitable comments about the efficiency of the staff in the Hôtel des Impôts, and admired the artificial jungle in the corridor. But my mind went back nearly sixty years to Spemann's laboratory in Freiburg, and how he had, for some specialised piece of research, produced newts with two heads but only a single stomach. The heads would fight to see which one could swallow a worm – which ended up in the same stomach space anyway. It could be stylised as a logo for the great French system of impôts, I thought, as I drove home to make out the cheque.

Up to our first April, we had come to recognise people by sight in our village, but apart from the mayor and his secretary,

Claudette, and Madame Cabanes – who was seldom seen – and the Belgian couple who kept the only shop in the village, we knew very few by name and between ourselves we used a collection of identifying names for them. There was Madame Loud-Mouth, and the Rabbit Lady – so called because when we paused to watch a 'ball-trap' shoot she had surprised us by asking in halting English the curious question 'What is the English for Rabbit?'

We were caught unprepared, and I suggested the answer 'Clay Pigeon'. Back home again I took to the Oxford Dictionary, but there was no Rabbit. The nearest was 'Rabat: Bands worn by priests etc.,' but I thought it unlikely that her question concerned ecclesiastical vestments.

Then we had Monsieur and Madame Grande Terrasse, and Monsieur and Madame Petite Terrasse, from the places where they lived. There was also Madame Golden Smile, and Monsieur Control, the eighty-year-old who during our absence went up to our house every day to see the progress. There was the Post mistress, and the *Cantonnier*, that individual in pill-box hat without which no French village would be complete. His job was to be the mayor's deputy in things physical such as sweeping the streets and removing weeds from the roadway, flushing the drains and the like. His real name was Cathala junior, Cathala senior being the man who had retired from the marine but was never seen without his service cap, and who, in intervals between his visits to the bistro at Argeliers, kept an impeccable allotment of flowers and vegetables in which one could not have found so much as the smallest seedling weed.

But now we began to know people. They invited us in, and we invited them. They admired enormously our décor and furnishing, so light and straightforward compared with their own. I wondered if our habit of leaving the shutters wide open might also spread.

One of the first we came to know intimately was short, stout, kindly, smiling Madame Rouanet, and it was when she came up to Ingrid one day, embraced her, and said with a beaming smile '*Vous êtes très bien adoptée, Madame,*' that we felt for the first time that we were local inhabitants. It was true. These kindly, generous people of our village had taken us into their community. We were both just as she had put it: *adopté*.

This did not happen immediately, although occasionally little straws would blow in the wind, as one day when we were walking up the lane toward the plateau. A tractor overtook us, but a little further up the hill stopped and backed down to us. The driver – it was M. Mompel, a wine-grower of course – stopped the tractor and turned round to us, his full-moon face radiating the friendliness we were beginning to find all around us.

'If you come a little higher up, you can see the sea,' he said. And then with an '*Allez!*' he drove on.

There were, however, two incidents which helped us a lot. The first was the fête of St. Baudile, which took place in May. The church, one of the smallest in France, stood absolutely on the summit of the hill behind the chateau, which was rather decayed but still showed where seething water could have been poured if necessary upon marauding Moors. (One often reads of molten lead being poured upon attackers by the beleaguered defenders of a fortress, but personally I doubt that so much lead was ready to hand in medieval times, or that vessels were on the battlements in which it could have been melted. Besides, why work with lead when a bucketful of boiling water would be just as discouraging to any attacker?)

Perched together on the summit of the village hill, it was as though the two establishments, the castle and the church, had their respective charge of the bodily and the spiritual care of the community below. The church was dedicated to Baudile or Baudilius, a non-canonized saint *honoris causa*, said to have been a Roman officer stationed at Nimes who were executed for the familiar treason of refusing to identify the contemporary emperor as God. His statue above the end of the nave was decidedly martial and ferocious, and no doubt like other martyrs he was a very determined man.

Baudile's Day was in mid-May, and always on a Sunday, and it was one of the occasions – along with Easter, Christmas, and All Souls – when we abandoned the temple and attended the mass in the village church. We liked the mass – it was simple, straightforward and surrounded by an atmosphere of sincerity and no-nonsense-from-the-Vatican, and our *curé*, M. Frioux, was a man we admired. He had been a social worker, so he had not lived a protected hot-house or monastic life, and knew very well what went on in the world. (There was no confessional cabinet in the church, I noticed.) He was a music lover and himself had a forceful well-pitched voice, and when he began to preach I could turn off my audio-amplifier. He happened to be a great traveller too, and he liked to organise trips to places like Lourdes, with suitable stops en route. He had even organised a bus journey to Rome so that the village people could actually meet the Pope for themselves. This was perhaps the only time that some of them had been outside the immediate surroundings, and he showed us pictures of the encounter in Rome itself. (The self-sufficiency of life in Montouliers often astonished me. One of the leading citizens astounded me by revealing that he had never realised that the water-course among the plane trees two miles distant in the plain was the Canal du Midi.)

Monsieur le Curé had three other villages under his wing, and that was one reason he was away like a rocket before the final Amen had died away. He had to do the mass elsewhere. But not on St. Baudile's Day. On that occasion he would conclude the service in his stentorian voice with: 'And now, it's time for an *apéritif*!'

The mass was well attended by the women, but by very few men. Apart from myself and the mayor, and young M. Rieussec who played the harmonium and who did so very well, there were only two other males. For this there were several reasons, we thought. A wine-grower was engaged in so ceaseless a war with ants, flies, weeds, mildew and other pests that he rarely had any spare time. Another reason, and one that applied to many other churches beside St. Baudile's, was that women have, I think, the task of carrying the heavy end of the log and are perhaps more sensitive to spiritual truths than are men. Women often trust God where their menfolk would prefer to have a grumbling session in the local pub. It is the women who keep the home, who do all the dull work of washing and sweeping, cooking and cleaning, and life can be very hard for them. They are often well aware of their need to charge up their batteries at the best source available.

On St. Baudile's Day the mass was special, and the little church was packed almost to capacity. The choir, ladies only, of three or four good singers was now supplemented by those of Cruzy and Quarante, with a choirmaster to conduct it. The entire service was choral, and it was refreshing to have a selection of really good tunes instead of the dismal self-mortifying dirges which we had to suffer at Narbonne's reformed church. (If ever I remarked that it was high time to throw out the hymnary, revised though it was as late as the 1970s, I found that others seemed entirely in agreement but in fact there was no better or less sin-orientated hymnal available.)

Thanks, glory, praise – that was what was in our hearts, and that was what we had at St. Baudile's – and Madame Audirac always managed to slip me a copy of the music so that I could help to swell by one male voice the volume of sound. The church itself was bright for the occasion, with a mass of red and white carnations at the foot of the altar table, and posies in the niches like a parish church in England on Easter Sunday. A row of night-lights in red saucers decorated the edge of the table, and a splendid bouquet of early gladioli flamed behind it.

In came the *curé* in his brilliant Pentecostal scarlet cope with gold-embroidered flames flickering up the sides and back. In attendance were six little angels-in-embryo, newly confirmed children who would be given odd jobs to do during the service such as handling the censer, taking up the offering, covering the empty chalice and so forth. They looked very serious and cherubic, and we liked to see them an hour later in jeans and T-shirt, pillion-riding round the village on mopeds.

After the service the congregation would stream out of the church and down the cobbled calade to the village centre-point at the bottom, and hurry along the street that led to the Salle des Réunions, a very spartan attempt at a village hall. The chairs had been cleared out, and down each side was a row of trestle tables behind which were ranged on the left the men so noticeably absent from the service, and on the right the ladies. The latter were selling home-made cakes and biscuits and pastries and crispy sugary things, all for the benefit of St. Baudile's Day. The men were not selling anything. They were dispensing the free aperitif. Red wine or white or rosé, *kir* of blackcurrant plain, or of *vrai Cassis de Dijon. Grenache*, light or dark. And, of course, *muscat*. And as it was now summertime, the *pastis* was allowed to join the other drinks.

We crowded into the hall and bought some pastries. The cakes had already gone, as cake-eating on Sunday afternoon regardless of cost is an anchor for the French family. In

Montouliers was almost as quiet as at midnight

Narbonne market we were often astonished at the speed with which cakes were sold at eighty, one hundred, or one hundred and twenty francs. We usually managed to raise a few dozen geraniums for this occasion, growing them in pots in the shelter of our cave, and these were quickly snapped up at a price I myself could never had dreamed of demanding. But the village ladies knew just how much they could get for good plants – and they got it.

On our first St. Baudile's Day we had not long been in the

Salle when I heard a voice. 'Monsieur Pilkington!' It was the mayor, beckoning me over to the male side to accept a glass of *grenache* which he poured out. I thanked him, and felt a glow of gratitude that went well with the tang of the excellent wine. 'And a glass for madame!'

In half an hour it was over. The mayor, the *curé*, the vintners, the women and ourselves were on our way up the street again, well aperitifed and carrying our bags of cakes and pastry. We dispersed to our houses. The sacred hour of lunch had arrived. Shutters were closed. Soon Montouliers was almost as quiet as at midnight, only a small group of youngsters remained opposite the *épicerie*, deep in earnest comparative motor-bikology.

At three o'clock the return to the Salle was more leisurely. The tables had now been cleared away and rows of chairs put out across the hall. We took our seats and the three o'clock programme began – at three-forty, for this was the Languedoc where people knew better than to be punctual like Parisians.

The afternoon entertainment varied. One year it was the *Ballons Rouges*, a teenage ballet group from Béziers who could have high-kicked and can-canned the Moulin Rouge over the moon – and seemed to have every intention of doing so. Another year it was their younger relatives, *Les Petits Raisins*. None of these boys and girls was older than ten, but they were so expertly made up and *maquillaged* that the illusion of their being youngish grown-ups was only broken when their school-master-trainer-compère made an entry and appeared a giant in comparison. It was astonishing to see how a ten-year-old girl could walk to and fro on the stage, microphone in hand, unabashed and confidently singing (in tune, too) the hits of the nineteen-twenties or nineteen-nineties with all the allure and husky-voiced mistinguettishness of an accomplished actress. I wondered whether one day we should see her name in lights in Montmartre, and whether she would then remember her public debut at Montouliers on St. Baudile's Day.

This occasion was one when St. Baudile happened to coincide with Mothers' Day, and Grandmothers' too. The producer asked Ingrid to come and sit near the front of the salle, and when one of the Raisins had sung her song of praise in honour of grandmas she jumped over the front of the boards and hopped up into Ingrid's lap, embracing her with kisses and a bouquet of red roses. It was a very charming tribute to be selected as the specimen grandmother of this happy and natural community.

The proceedings finished (except for the dance until midnight for those who still had the energy to be there) with the drawing of the tickets for the tombola. Madame Rouanet had been up to the house to sell us tickets, and others had sold them in the surrounding villages, so that the number disposed of at five francs apiece ran to more than two thousand. The prizes were all laid out on the table, and they included some very worthwhile items too – a whole smoked ham, a microwave oven, and various gifts in kind from tradesmen who had the local people among their customers. There were also one or two pieces of really beautiful lace, the work of older women in the villages, and I could not help thinking – especially after we drew one in the Cruzy tombola – that this was perhaps the last generation that would ever see such wonderful handywork.

On the occasion of a tombola for which one has dutifully bought tickets I am usually glad that when the next prize is held up the ticket is not mine. And so I was on this first occasion. And then a little girl drew the next number out of the box and it was one of Ingrid's.

'Madame Pilkington!' Ingrid stepped over the legs of her neighbours and walked toward the front to receive her prize. I was delighted. Everyone would now recognise her and know who she was – the lady from Les Cactus with the difficult name was identifiable at last.

There was great applause. People were actually glad that she had drawn a prize. She was one of them. And the prize was one of which we could never complain, a jug and six glasses, and three bottles of Soureilhan rouge, with the compliments of the Co-operative Viticole de Montouliers. Yes, we had arrived, and landed in a happy, genuine, welcoming community.

It was in September that the other event took place which helped to establish that even if we frequently went back to legendary countries such as Jersey and Sweden, we really belonged right there in our Languedocian village of Montouliers in the sunny, easy-going Minervois. People in the village were startled on this particular morning when they opened their copies of *L'Indépendent*, the daily paper on sale at the grocery, and saw a photograph of their own newly-attached villager actually being dubbed a Chevalier de la Confrérie du Minervois, by the Grand Master. It was the first time that this distinction had been given to anyone from the village, as some of the ladies told us, almost beside themselves with pride.

It had happened in this way. I had written several articles about some of the more interesting facets of the Minervois area, and these had duly appeared in the *Sunday Telegraph*. I had shown copies to Christian and Ginette Bonnel, both of whom were in the Confrérie; and Christian, who was the Honorary Clerk, had recommended to the Court of the Confrérie that I should be made a Chevalier on account of my services to the Minervois. I had not mentioned this within the village, as I did not really want to sing my own praises.

On the fateful day we drove over to the Chateau d'Auriac, outside the ancient fortified cité of Carcassone. I was dressed in my best – and what was my best had been the object of considerable discussion over lunch. I was not one for wearing a suit except when it was *de rigueur*, as was the case with City Livery Companies in London. So I had no suit at all in France. If no suit, then what? Throughout the summer I wore shorts and an open shirt, condescending, however, to wear a pair of clean, light trousers if invited out or going to a concert, where the French were always so scrupulously tidy, well-coiffed and perfumed – and where I consequently wore a tie to be in harmony. This was not just for Ingrid's sake but because I was jealous of the reputation of the homeland.

It was important not be to regarded as under- nor as over-dressed. In the end, we decided that a respectable blue blazer, suitably embellished with the Rugby School arms on the pocket and the smart buttons of the Royal Swedish Yacht Club would fit the bill.

The Chateau d'Auriac was a stately home with a capital 'S', marble floors and all, and it was now a hotel, just the kind of hotel I would like to stay in if I were sure that someone else would pull out their American Express card to settle my account. I had been brought up in a non-conformist Lanca-shire home, and both there and later at Rugby the doctrine had been implicit: that one should leave ostentation and extrava-gance to others. For quite different reasons – an overdose of ostentation, perhaps – Ingrid felt the same; we were a great pair for looking at prices, as we would rather give money away than pay for services which were needlessly expensive. We had several times walked within hailing distance of the famous La Baumanière restaurant at Les Baux and then sat among the scrub of cystus and rosemary to lunch on bread and pâté and a can of beer. So we were ready to contemplate the Chateau d'Auriac, but would never have dreamed of staying there.

The Chateau was also a training school for good quality hotel staff, and the young things spotlessly turned out and yet nervous to make the slightest mistake in front of the maître d'hôtel gave the place a subdued elegance. The house stood in superb and rather English grounds with magnificent cedars and other specimen trees, a lake with swans, just as though it were in England, and the more French feature of a grotto with trickling water and wet moss and an unidentified classical statue, near which was a sort of dell in which rows of chairs had been set facing a piece of lawn backed by trees and a hedge. It reminded me at once of the setting for *A Midsummer Night's Dream* in Regents Park.

We were correctly dressed, and we took our places in one of the rows of seats. Some medieval heralds with standards hanging from their long trumpets stepped out from between the bushes and blew a fanfare. The Grand Master and wardens and the court came in and took their places on the stage of lawn. They were dressed in flowing robes of a sort of off-wine shade, as though some milk had been added to the rouge. Their caps of the same colour were more like brimless toppers. It was all very splendid, and it reminded me of such a City scene in London as the election of sheriffs.

Another fanfare, and three men in blue and scarlet gowns marched in, swept their soft and broad hats in a low bow to the Grand Master, then stood to one side. They were there as representatives of the Confrérie of the Corbières. Another fanfare, and others came in. And another, and so on. In their splendid gowns they edged the lawn, the guild men of one wine-growing area after another: Carcassonne, Fitou, Rivesaltes, Narbonne, La Clape and its surroundings, Limoux. They were like a Shakespearian pageant.

We applauded. Another fanfare, and the Grand Master opened the proceedings. Then he turned to Christian Bonnel who doffed his cap and gave a very well thought-out and amusing if rather flattering account of me and my alleged

I took a sip, and tried to look contemplative

services to the Minervois. He put the paper back in his pocket. By very good fortune I had been as an outside spectator to a similar function held in the Palace of the Archbishops in Narbonne, so I knew what would be expected of me. I stepped out, bowed low before the Grand Master, and took three steps to the side.

A member of the court approached with a silver tray on which were two glasses and two bottles of this year's wine – that is, from the *vendanges* of the year before. One was red, one white. I picked up each bottle in turn, scrutinised the labels, tried to look very knowledgeable and wise, and opted for the white. A glass was poured for me.

I knew just how to proceed. I turned to half face the audience. All eyes were upon me now, and Ingrid was taking a photograph. I took a sip, rolled my lips from side to side and tried to look contemplative. Another sip, then another. Up with the eyebrows, on with the smile of satisfaction. I held the glass up high.

'*Excellent!*' I cried.

There was applause, I tossed back the remainder of the wine, and put the glass back on the tray before turning again to the Grand Master.

Christian, who seemed to combine the offices of clerk and beadle, handed the Master a staff which ended in the pruned stock of a vine. I half knelt and was dubbed on each shoulder and formally declared a Chevalier of the Confrérie. I bowed low again, and Ginette Bonnel, one of those rare birds, a lady liveryman of the Confrérie, stepped forward and placed round my neck the badge of a chevalier which was hung from an olive green ribbon. She handed me the scroll signed by the Grand Master, and I walked backwards to withdraw. Again I was thankful that I had seen such a ceremony elsewhere. That, seasoned with some know-how as a past master of the Worshipful Company of Glass Sellers, saw me through.

Five super-selected Paris chefs followed in turn. Their services were, no doubt, to see that Minervois wines figured on the recommended wine lists. As dark began to fall, we adjourned to the lower terrace for a splendid dinner in which the super cooks had, I believe, had a finger. Wine unlimited, handshakes, embraces for the Bonnels, and it was time to head for home.

Of all the handful of newly dubbed chevaliers, the only one whose portrait appeared in the *Indépendent*, twisting his mouth and looking exceedingly enigmatic, was myself. As soon as one of our village ladies saw it there was almost a stampede to get a copy from the *épicerie*. Yes, there he was, this strange elderly Englishman who had come to their village. Their Chevalier! I think it was Ingrid's record day for kisses received. It was our village, and we were honoured to belong to it.

8

The Denizens

The cliff, and the broad hole which was the entrance to our cave (not *our* entrance, but our interior, as we had been told) was a striking feature of the approach to the village from the direction of Bize, and in our early days we had considered the possibility of lighting it from within. It would give a pleasant and at the same time rather mysterious effect, we thought, and it was something that could easily be installed by myself. And then we wondered. Was it really such a good idea after all? Was it perhaps not just that sort of embellishment which might destroy the natural beauty of the place? And who would appreciate it anyway?

During recent years there had been a gradual decline in the population as families became smaller and the younger generation sought other work elsewhere rather than be tied to the village vine-stock. Not so long ago, and certainly within the memory of those in their fifties, the village had supported three cafés, and I myself knew where they had been. Étienne's own house had been one of them, there was a second on the Route de Bize, the street leading westward out of the town. The third was easily identified by the faded word '*Billiard*' over the door of a now deserted house on the street leading up to our lane. But now, with a population stated in the annual give-away calendar of the PTT as only one hundred and eighty-six, no café could hope to survive on ministering to the needs of the small number of men who would patronise it, for every sensible villager either had his own wine or drew plonk in a plastic can from the co-operative, or both. Indeed, there seemed to be only one man who liked to sit in a pub over a glass of beer, and this he did daily at La Terrasse, the surviving café in the neighbouring and larger village of Argeliers.

With no café, no restaurant, and the blessing of no through traffic, the only people still in Montouliers after dark were the villagers themselves. They lived behind closed shutters, and even if they had not done so their houses were so placed that not more than three had even a distant view of our cave. Any floodlighting could only be for the benefit of visitors, of which there were none except in the summer, when it was too light in the late evening to floodlight the place to any purpose. No, we would not light the cave. And no doubt the denizens, who much preferred the darkness, were greatly relieved by our decision.

That birds lived on the ledges was obvious enough from the mass of guano on parts of the rock face, and from the scatter of sixty-seven furry grey pellets on the sandy ground under the lip of the mouth. Obviously, these were regurgitated by an owl, and most probably by a barn owl, although there was no 'tuwhit-tuwhooing' at night. It is always interesting – and very often surprising – to see exactly what has been sicked up, and sometimes I would take a pellet and place it under a stone in a dish of water until it was thoroughly soaked and the contents could be teased out with a pair of needles. Among other odds and ends there were the sharp, curving teeth of voles and the ribs and thigh-bones of small rodents. A selection of these bones found their place eventually in the new sales parlour of the wine co-operative. I noticed that many of the pieces cut off vine-stocks in the winter pruning had shapes which were in one way or another suggestive as natural sculptures, and I converted a few into curious objects which were on display to amuse the customers. There was Miss Montouliers, and the Grandmère de Miss Montouliers, suitably clothed in odds and ends from the rag-bag, and one piece which at once brought to mind the fearful Tarasque of Tarascon was labelled '*Le Monstre de Montouliers; mange jeunes filles*'. Some of the small rodent bones were dropping appropriately from his mouth or were glued to the stand underneath his jaws. For the Tarasque was a messy eater.

I asked Étienne what other bird inhabited the cave, and he replied that it was a '*oiseau de nuit*'. Further identification was not offered, and maybe could not be. But on several summer evenings a fairly large bird would come whiffling through the gap where the path led to the cave, sweeping over the terrace to

109

vanish in the dusky twilight of the copse near our gate. We knew what this bird was, too. By its size, its curious call and its peculiarly swift and twisting flight there was no doubt that it was a nightjar.

There was also a family of rabbits. The floor of the cave was not very hard, and there was a burrow from which mother rabbit brought out a quantity of bedding material when she set about spring cleaning. Étienne put some stones over the entrance, which merely meant that a new burrow was begun a yard or two away. Now and again we saw a very small rabbit which had come out and had found a hiding place from the soaking given by the Bas Rhône irrigation, crouching in the wet grass behind a cactus. I am not especially fond of rabbits, but I was sad when I found the back half of the body of this little one on the lawn one morning, neatly bitten through, probably by an itinerant fox.

We had, of course, more than enough visits from non-resident rabbits. They liked to nibble the tender leaves and buds of the young vines. The only way to deal with this nuisance was to buy for the plants stockings of plastic netting about fifteen inches high, and these bright blue defences gave a very cheerful appearance to the vineyard and – to judge by the droppings – made the rabbits change their menu to take instead the lower leaves of older stocks. That was quite a useful service as it achieved a sort of summer pruning, but I still regarded the rabbits with disfavour. On the other hand, when myxomatosis spread across our part of the Minervois we were not particularly pleased. The sight of rabbits sitting in the road, feeble and nervous wrecks, unable to move if a rare car came over the hill, was a nasty one.

Rabbits could do harm to vineyards, and even more to vegetable gardens. There was a small population of them in the rough country and, of course, they liked to run along the little tracks which led from one patch of vineyards to another. Probably it was their relatives that had made these paths in the first place. Sometimes when out exploring the *garrigue*, I would come across a small heap of dry sticks or broken stems of rosemary in the path, which concealed a snare. I have never liked the business of snaring, and my first tendency was to pull the snare out, or cut the wire of the noose, but after a while I realised that it was not really my business to interfere with

Our cave gave shelter to bats, both large and small

rabbit-catching when there was no doubt that rabbits were destructive and also could provide a good meal for a village family – but certainly never for me. The mere smell of rabbit flesh was something that always revolted me, taking me back to the dissections of early days in zoology classes when one had the creatures spread out crucified on baking boards. So I left the snares alone. But it is a curious fact that although I have seen snares in the area over a period of several years, I have never once seen a noose with a rabbit in it; nor, which is even more strange, have I seen anyone setting or inspecting the snares which keep on turning up in the little pathways over the heathy land.

Perhaps it was a Beatrix Potter hangover from my youth that made me somewhat tolerant of rabbits. I liked them to feel at home in our cave. And, of course, they were not the only denizens. Our cave gave shelter to bats both large and small, and sometimes a small bird would dart in and make a swift surveying tour of the cavern at such a breathlessly high speed that I never had a chance to identify it. Of course, there were spiders too, and when first we took over the property there was a colony of bees whose pendant comb was far overhead at the entrance. But not for ever. Bees are clever creatures, but they are unable to calculate the amount of comb which can safely be hung from the rock. Eventually there is a disaster, and the ants make a swift job of emptying the fallen combs of honey, leaving to the lizards the juicy meal of grubs.

Sometimes on a crisp night of cold, and starlit sky, we would walk through the tunnel of cypresses to the cave, and look out from beneath the natural, stalagmitic portal across the *vallon* to where the lights shone in distant villages and fifteen miles away the floodlit mass of the great cathedral of St. Just at Narbonne stood out alone against the dim backdrop of the headland of La Clape. It was strange that nothing else of a city the size of Narbonne was to be seen, except when there were low clouds and a pinkish orange glow upon their underside indicated that there was indeed plenty of street lighting to reflect. St. Just stood on its private hill very much at the top of Narbonne, and the intervening ranges of lower hills conveniently cut off the rest of the view to hide all but the cathedral itself.

Standing in the cave mouth could give one a curiously troglodytic sensation, especially as the cave had been lived in long ago. Long ago – yes, but how long? To say, as people did, that it was maybe one hundred and fifty thousand years ago was to me quite meaningless, for what was a score of thousands more or less? I had never been able to understand why the events and ages in the history of our Earth were habitually reckoned in multiples of three hundred and sixty-five revolutions of the planet at its speed of the moment. That system might be good enough for putting a dinner date in ones diary, but such a railway-timetable list of dates and times was useless when dealing with the wonder of the creation, the fantastically ingenious structure of the Earth and the evolution of its admirable crew of living creatures – let alone the universe known and unknown. Certainly when looking out from the entrance of the cave and thinking of those who once had lived there I found it much more reasonable to think of time in G-years, God-years, which are simply a log-to-the-base-10 figure, rather than the more fashionable linear years.

Of course, this is my own equally arbitrary system of measurement of time and I cannot claim any authority for it. Indeed, I should not really call the units God-years. God obviously works outside the dimension of time altogether. But G-years, if we may so call them, are a way of looking at the world which robs it of the absurd sort of academic calculation that if we had the world's history written with only ten lines to every thousand years, the volumes would occupy four hundred feet of library shelving and the whole course of civilisation would be found only on the two sides of the last page (to date) of the final volume – a real *reductio ad absurdum* if ever there was one.

I think it was the sheer beauty of the Minervois and Corbières countryside that always brought these thoughts to my mind. The astounding wonder and ingenuity of the creative genius was there on every hand. The mighty plane trees, the intricate chemical structure of the anthocyanins which formed in the autumn leaves of the vines and caused the breath-taking sensation of colour mediated to me by the magic of the millions of fibres running from the rear of a pair of retinas to disappear in the brain. The soft, wind-worn shapes of the folded hills backed by the jagged snow-capped heights of the Pyrenees; the fluttering flight of a bee-eater darting with a flash of green and red from its perch on a telephone wire to snatch a bee in its curved bill; the extraordinary fact that two simple elements could be combined to make water, colourless (except in the canal, perhaps) and ubiquitous, without which the bold and brilliantly planned invention of life would be impossible.

By my system of calculation our cave was lived in five years ago. (The end of World War II would be about one and a half, Luther two and a half, Moses three and a half, and our first inhabitants of Montouliers five – a mere four years later than the first live combinations of elements in the primeval seas.)

It was not much of a house, our cave. It must have been like the Underneath-the-Arches dwellings of Charing Cross, a shelter from wind and rain, sleet and snow. Perhaps this larger cave and the smaller one round the corner of the bluff were nothing more than crude shelters, although those who lived there might have thought of them as highly desirable residences, *faute de mieux*. And probably *mieux* could not have been found, at least no nearer than the Grotte de Bize, which was also lived in during those times.

The paleolithic inhabitants would have been hunters, and probably they had little time for anything else. Cultivation had not been invented and so far as I know they were not artists. There was no sign of strip cartoons of animals or early Asterix characters on the walls. The shelter probably had a fire at the entrance for cooking and heat and light, but I doubted whether their life was much other than one of hunting, cooking, eating, sleeping, and going out to hunt again next day. Life may have been hard, or it may not, but as it was the only life to be lived it

113

seems unlikely that any would have said to themselves, with a simple Cro-Magnon sigh, 'There must be better things in life than this,' though it is just possible that some individual, frowning a furrow across his not very high forehead, could have wondered in a simple, enigmatic way what life was for. Was it a prelude to something else?

Did they have any beliefs, these early residents? We would never know, because beliefs cannot be dug up and put in a showcase. Only cult objects are imperishable, but the fact that there were none to be found from those early days tells us nothing beyond the fact that cult objects were not found, or conceivably did not exist. But we liked to feel that there was laughter, and talk, and children's games in that cave, and that, like ourselves, the older ones might walk to the entrance and see the sun edging up over the hills to the eastward and feel such a sense of thankfulness that their eyes, like ours, were moist with gratitude for the loveliness of life.

And then it would be time to stop dreaming and get back to work, to the hunting and cooking and tool-making; and maybe with a cover of wet leaves on the fire they could smoke out those bees in the roof and let the young ones have a treat of honey and perhaps locusts too. Even now there are occasional locusts to be found in the vineyards, and the somewhat larger Egyptian grasshopper is not uncommon either.

Food and water were the essentials. The *ruisseau du village* below the cave may well have had more water then than now, for today it is usually bone dry. Not far away and under the rock in the corner of the Real orchard there is a spring which flows for four or five months in the year and may earlier have been more constant. Washing? Well, why should one wash when the wild animals did not? Except some of the birds. They liked to flutter and splutter in pools of rainwater after a shower.

But food – that was vital. Vegetables were easy enough, and wild asparagus still grows today in the cave, a sure sign of water somewhere in the rock. Wild leeks and onions are abundant across the *garrigue*, and herbs of all kinds are available within a minute's walk. Thyme, sage, fennel and rosemary, everything was to hand to add flavour as the early French chefs prepared the main course of venison, and maybe of small wild horses. There could have been eels, and perhaps trout and clams in the Cesse, the fish taken in various ways – with hooks of thorn or bone, or sometimes by women lying in the stream and squeezing out their own body milk to lure the *friture*. And, of course, wild boar, as difficult to hunt then as they are today. Probably smaller mammals could be snared but the larger and fleeter ones were best hunted by a communal expedition which rounded them up and drove them ahead into some situation from which there was no escape, as at the rock of Solutré near Mâcon, where bison, deer and wild horses were pursued to the smoothing-iron tip of the rock from which there was only one escape – a frightened scream or bellow as the creatures hurtled over the precipice edge, bouncing from rock to rock to land crushed and bleeding at the side of the hearths where the women gutted and skinned them and butchered the joints to roast and smoke them at the fire. The remains of more than a hundred thousand horses slaughtered in the primitive *boucherie chevaline* of Solutré have been counted. But the site was lived in for a long time, and bringing it down to scale this seemingly huge boneyard would be produced by an average of only two horses a week. Sometimes I wondered if our crag was used for the same purpose. It might have been, for the shape is suitable enough, though the evidence is lacking.

Perhaps the girls and boys brought in the herbs. They still do so in the village today. Rosemary and fennel would have been excellent for disguising the taste of meat that was becoming a bit flyblown. And, of course, there was fruit in due season. Blackberries maybe, and wild apples, and nuts in abundance. I doubt if the people of our cave ever died of hunger or deficiency diseases. Accidents and broken limbs were more likely causes.

Already the land was an embryo France, so there would have been snails too, with garlic, just as there are today, when a heavy rain will bring the village people up the lane to hunt along our bank. Delicious, but troublesome to prepare. I suspect our cave-dwellers just put them on hot stones to cook, and pulled out the spiral bodies with their fingers or a splinter of bone.

Not many of the public came to look at the cave to which, as it was *classé*, there was a right of access. Those few who did were much more curious to see us than the cave, except for the rare school classes. The children had to file across the terrace, and Ingrid would give each of them a toffee, adding a little lesson of her own about deportment, that if there were thirty-two children she had to have thirty-two toffee papers handed in when they returned on their way out. And as I often found the teachers to be much better at discipline than at pre-history, I would usually go to the cave with the children and try to imagine with them what Cro-Magnon times were like. But modern children have little sense of time, even the Thomas Cook variety. And many who know all about working a computer cannot do the simplest sums. Yet the classes were always extremely well behaved.

One Sunday the village was the subject of a visit by fifty members of the Society for the Discovery of the Languedoc, a fairly learned society based in Montpellier and consisting partly of people from the university – one of whom pointed out to me some fossil vegetation in the stones of the church tower which I had not previously noticed. It was a winter's day, when the Tramontane was demonstrating that it could do fifty miles an hour at zero temperature without the least trouble, but the guests bravely visited the cobbled calades, inspected the chateau-fort and the church, wandered down to see the curious water-conduit of the Romans which was later used as a horse-trough and now provided a very romantic bower for young couples in the balmy evenings of spring. Then they all came up to the cave and I tried to imagine for them what life was like in the days of the not-so-stupid men of Neanderthal type. And it was interesting to find that the scientists in the group, like all others I had met, suffered from the same illusion about the Neanderthal.

It is usual for a teacher, or text-book writer, to try to show off his slight knowledge of German by saying that Neanderthal means, of course, the valley of the Neander River, not far from Düsseldorf. This error is repeated in every text book I have ever seen, and it is curious to discover that the authors have not the initiative to look at a map of the area, from which they would quickly discover that the river in the gorge of which the remains of hominids were found is not the Neander but the Düssel, a brook upon which the *dorf* of the name stands. There is in fact no River Neander, but the story of how the Neanderthaler got his name is interesting enough.

Long ago there lived in the Rhineland a young visionary who betook himself to the cliffs of the Düssel brook and lived there as a hermit. He was somewhat like the prophets of old, and when the thunderclouds came rolling across from the plain of the Rhine and the lightning flashed over the countryside he would run out and stand upon the cliff and cry 'My Father, my Father, I see his chariot of fire, and his horses. I rejoice – for though the mountains may quake and the hills fall down, his covenant is unbreakable, his mercy endures for ever!'

The young man was a notable hymn-writer, and perhaps the most familiar to the English churchgoer is his *'Lobe den Herren, den mächtigen König der Erde'* (Praise to the Lord, the Almighty the King of Creation), sung to that splendid tune, *Stralsund*. One Whitsunday he stood upon the crag above the brook as another great storm spread over the land where now the Mannesmann tube factory stands, glorying excitedly in the majesty of the forces of nature. Three days later he collapsed and died. That was in 1680. He was only thirty years of age, but the people of the area had come to love him, and the craggy bend in the Düssel gorge came at once to be known after him.

The young visionary was named Joachim Neander. He was to be remembered in the name of Neander's gorge, or Neanderthal, which has remained ever since. But it was two centuries later that a quarryman discovered some bones in a narrow cave in the cliff where Neander had once seen so vividly the magnificence of his Father in Heaven.

Beyond the cave our domaine continued for another fifty yards or so round the corner of the bluff to spread as a flattish shelf about twenty feet across and mainly of bare limestone with a scatter of rosemary and lavender and, of course, with pine-needles fallen from the pines miraculously growing on the steep side of the cliff. I knew where our boundary was even if it was not marked in any way, the mayor having tactfully indicated through a third party that I should take away the little *propriété privé* notice I had originally put on a stake to mark where our land began. I had only done this to deter shooters, but I at once understood that anything which might be interpreted as ostentatious ownership was quite out of place in our village, and that nobody would come trespassing either. Boundaries were free and easy and existed more on the plans in the *Mairie* than in fact.

Round the corner, the rock fell almost vertically to a pair of vegetable patches, but straight ahead along the flat was a pinewood, and even if its frontage was very narrow, it was the one sole direction from which a fire could reach us. For this reason we were very particular about keeping this shelf of land free of dead grass or shrubs, or too well provided with pine-needles. More than that, I had laid a three-quarter inch flexible pipe along the area, connected to the Bas Rhône irrigation supply, and in dangerously dry weather I would put a sprinkler on the end of it and wet the whole area and the nearer pines as well.

One hot day in June I smelled smoke, and, running to look beyond the cave, I found flames curling over the edge from the allotments below and the dead grass and the lavender bushes on our land already alight. Thanks to the presence of the water-pipe it did not take me more than a minute to make our land safe, and then I could turn my attention to the cause of the fire. A youngish woman had done a van der Born, raking together a great heap of tinder and setting it alight. As the nearest water supply for her vegetable garden was some way distant at the old horse trough, she could not control the fire at all. A lad was running off to fill a bucket for her, but I found it more effective to fill one of our pails from the irrigation lead above.

The blaze had been seen by Monsieur Boillon, an energetic and former military man who lived beyond the *vallon*. He at once jumped on his moped, quickly reached the lane by the vegetable patches, leaped off and scaled the rock like a commando attacking a fortress. In a moment he was up beside me, insisting on taking the bucket and hurling the water down on the fire. Sometimes, I noticed, the throw went a bit wild and instead of landing in the bonfire went smack in the face of the lady who had lit the blaze. He smiled. So did I. She had already had a few pailfuls from myself before he arrived.

Between the two of us we quickly had the fire doused, and the lady along with it, but the event showed the wisdom of having the Bas Rhône supply spread throughout our land. And we had been fortunate, too, that this was not one of the days when pressure had fallen to zero because of work on the pumping system many miles away.

That evening, four of the villagers came up to sit on the terrace, and say how cretinous cretins could be, especially over lighting fires.

118

I agreed. A glass of *grenache*, perhaps?

Volontiers!

It was a wonderful thing to feel this warmth of concern and affection always around us.

9

Creatures Great and Small

Our cave also contained a curiosity in the form of scores of tiny craters in the dusty sand of the floor. These were less than an inch across and perfectly circular, and the shape of an inverted cone. If I smoothed over the floor to fill them up they would return overnight, and Étienne said they were caused by particles of rock falling off the ceiling. But I disproved this. If one dropped a particle heavily enough to make such a hole then it should be left at the bottom of the crater, very much like a giant meteorite on the surface of the earth; yet the craters were empty.

I excavated the craters carefully, hoping to find ant-lions – which make exactly such holes. But I never found a creature hidden at the bottom. Then one day I noticed the tiny footmarks of a small bird. The craters were peck marks, but who did the pecking remained a mystery. Presumably it was some creature hunting for ants. The only small bird I definitely identified there was an ortolan, which had broken its neck in colliding with the wall.

The cave was not the only habitation for wild life. There was our end of the postal system too. Madame Real had used as a mail-box an old shoe box which she stood in the front of the open garage or car-shelter. She had written *Courrier* on the side, and cut a slit in the lid. It seemed that the postman was quite ready to bring his bright little yellow van up the drive to deposit her mail in it, and when we had taken over the house I placed a mail-box in close proximity, but on the side of the house. For a week or two our mail, supplemented usually by several copies of the advertising material the PTT had undertaken to deliver, was put there as before, but eventually the *postier* declared in a kind but authoritative way that this could not continue. Our mail-box should be at the entry to the domaine. The reason was probably that he could formerly turn his little Renault van in front of the garage because Madame Real had no car, and if anything cluttered up the space it would probably be the scantily bikinied sylph in a hamoc. But now that we had arrived, the fairway was cluttered by a Volvo and our own Renault Quatre as well. That meant that he had to drive all the way down the curving driveway, *marche arrière*, and that was not without its dangers. So the Pilks had to move their letter-box.

I put the box on a stout stake at the entry, and at mid-morning coffee-time Ingrid or I would walk down to see what had arrived. And it was thus that we came to know French Polly.

Her full name was *Pollistes gallica*, and she was a solitary wasp. She had very sensibly chosen the letter-box as an ideal situation in which to build a highly desirable residence for her young ones. There were only two or three to start with, but her hexagon-building and egg-laying went very much hand in hand, and finally there were twenty-three cells in an oval cluster, secured to a neat stalk.

It was a delight to watch Polly at work. The letter-box was one that had a flap at the top through which the letters were put, and the whole of the front was hinged to swing open when the latch was turned with a screw-driver. This door had a broad slit near the bottom, originally covered by a piece of transparent plastic, so that one could see if there was any mail. Plastics of that kind are not used to the brilliant sun of the Minervois, so it had become brittle and eventually fell to pieces. That was Polly's chance, and she chose the right-hand bottom corner near the back. This was curious, as her family habit was to build a nest hanging from a neat little stalk, but Polly changed this system and built sideways, the stalk attached to the wall of the box near the bottom. This was an originality which was nearly her undoing when the *postier* dropped *The Economist* through the flap and one or two cells close to the edge were broken. However, she soon mended them. She was an expert builder.

I am not sure where she got her materials. There was so much to be found and taken from dead branches, bark, vine stalks, even the wooden underside of the eaves. She scraped away somewhere or other with her jaws and flew back to the

121

mail-box, chewing all the while like a security guard at London Airport. The result was, of course, a material much like unbleached newsprint, and Polly's sticky saliva was a wonderful substance for cementing everything together. When I first discovered her activity, she had completed the delicate but strong stalk and was beginning to lay out the walls of the first cells. She never minded my inspecting the works, but some of her children were less amenable. Perhaps the postman had dumped too much supermarket junk mail on them.

French Polly was ceaselessly active, laying, feeding, building and cleaning up. The cells became roofed over and shortly afterward the first members of Polly's brood began to come out, biting their way through the capping of their cells. We would open the door of the box, take out the mail, and admire her family before we closed it again.

After a while we became worried for Polly's safety. Heavy items of mail were often being thrust through the slit in the top, falling on top of Polly's exquisite stalked nest. We did not want the wasps to be disturbed, and we had no wish that the *postier* should be stung while going about his lawful business. We, of course, had to open the door of the box to get at the mail, and if we tended to collect the letters with lightning rapidity and then slam the door, it was all part of the thrill of having Polly choose our very own box for her building site.

So, although Polly was harmless enough, we were anxious to warn the *postier* and his holiday stand-in-lady that there was by this time quite an active colony of wasps flying in and out of the slit, and that to open the box could be somewhat hazardous to anyone of a nervous temperament. We put a notice '*Attention! Guêpes!*' on the box, thinking that this would result in Polly and her brood being left in peace. At the foot of the post we also placed a grocer's fruit-box suitably marked with an arrow and the word '*Courrier*'.

Next day our mail was placed in the fruit tray and no doubt the wasps, which by now included a few very vigorous young adults, were much relieved that the daily tip-and-run visitation of the *postier* had now stopped. But before the week was out, tragedy struck in the form of Monsieur Ruisseau.

Monsieur Ruisseau lived close by. He had been born and bred in the next village but he had become a townee in Béziers and only spent half his time in Montouliers, where he pruned his mulberries and got ready to return to Béziers two days later. His visits to our village were regular, and not particularly noticeable, for though friendly enough in a negative way, he took no part in any of the local activities. Not even, I believe, in the parish bingo.

Monsieur Ruisseau came walking up our drive one morning and rang the bell. He had our fruit-box and our mail with him and he handed it over.

'It is not necessary to be afraid of wasps,' he declared with the self-conscious omniscience of a school teacher pointing out a well-known and obvious fact to a particularly stupid pupil. 'It is only necessary to spray them with a suitable preparation. There are many to be had in the shops.'

He evidently thought I had never seen a wasp before; and as far as *Pollistes gallica* was concerned he was most probably right.

'But I have, of course, such materials. So I have sprayed the nest in your letter-box, and now it is quite safe.'

Quite safe! Poor Polly and her children all murdered by this chemical warfare fiend! I was speechless.

Monsieur Ruisseau fortunately assumed that I was so overcome with gratitude that I was unable to find suitable words in which to express my thanks to him for his selfless and unstinted service.

'Ah!' he said comfortingly. '*C'est rien.*'

Rien! And that beautiful, delicately-built nest ruined by his ham-handed efforts at neighbourliness! I murmured something about how thoughtful he was, and how grateful we were, and a lot more clap-trap of a suitable kind.

Monsieur Ruisseau was pleased, even if I did not reward his valour with a glass of grenache. He bowed a little, and departed. As soon as he was out of sight I ran to the letter-box and opened it, hoping perhaps that letting in the breezy air might still salvage something.

But it was too late. Polly and her children lay there, dead.

My attitude toward Polly was perhaps illogical, but from days far back in the zoology labs I had a way of regarding other creatures which, to some people, may have seemed rather odd. I knew enough about evolution – not the mechanism, because theories on that subject were changing more frequently than Agatha Christie plays at a London theatre – and perhaps my feeling that our habitual time-scale was rather ridiculous made the facts of evolutionary change more real and ever-present. A text-book evolutionary tree spread out over hundreds of millions of years robbed even the Ichthyosaurus, whose bones I had collected when at school, of all reality. The fishes of the Permian, poor old Archaeopteryx like an umbrella overtaken by a hurricane, the early mammals, even the hominids dug up by the Leakeys in Kenya, these seemed hopelessly remote. It was much easier if one thought in G- years to realise that they were rather recent sidesteps off the main line leading to man. To myself. It had been an astonishingly brilliant idea to produce man through genetic mutation and selection, but man was not the sole inheritor, as many people were now beginning to realise. Why else should they be worried about marmosets if the paper and furniture industries were thriving on the remains of their habitat? Surely because the fact of kinship was dimly or in some cases very acutely felt. And rightly so.

To me, animals living or extinct were creatures over whose pain and death man had been allowed to climb to his own birth, and to torment and slaughter them, as overdressed Spanish torreadors liked to do was, I felt, to fling their evolutionary suffering in their faces. (I admit to having cheered when I saw one of these heroes gored and trampled to death in front of the television cameras.) But one had to try to strike a balance. I was happy one day in Narbonne to see a frog hopping down the middle of the main shopping street and to have had the chance to run after him and catch him before a car could run him over, and then to carry him down to the canal and drop him in the bubbly outfall below the weir. Anyone with an ounce of regard for animals would have done the same. But the fact remained that many evolved creatures had qualities which were admirable for their own protection and flourishing, but which I could not accept that we had always to preserve. Ingrid shared these views, so we had an unofficial and not very logical list in our minds of creatures which we might slosh or squash. It included wasps, if a pest at mealtimes, mosquitoes, several types of fly (but not my old genetics assistant *Drosophila*, the fruit-fly), and hornets under all circumstances. Moths, beetles, centipedes and the like were preserved. So were birds, and snakes. I always regarded snakes as, at worst, fairly harmless and, at best, good friends to the gardener. When, one day, we were sitting in the square at Ax-les-Thermes, a pleasant little snake came out from under one of the seats, and a rather hysterical woman tried to jump on it. When I asked her why, because surely it only had *une seule vie, exactement comme vous-même madame,* she looked at me in a rather puzzled way; and meanwhile the snake escaped.

Polly was a wasp, admittedly, but she was more concerned with her family than with getting into the honey-pot at tea-time. I liked and respected her. But hornets, no. They were a nuisance, and dangerous, and they were on our hit list as were also, and inevitably, the various pests of the vine, aphids on the roses, and pine processionaries. And slugs. I never had qualms about putting down metaldehyde to kill slugs. The production of slugs seemed to me a case of evolution having gone off the rails. But on the whole it was true that – if only they realised it – any creature that was not a noxious nuisance or wildly destructive like the *loirs* at Soleil d'Oc could feel perfectly safe within the bounds of our domaine. They were part of our family, and would be treated as such.

During the winter months most of these friends were dormant, or at least unobtrusive, but the squirrels continually reminded us of their presence. Blessed with our special climate they had no need to hibernate and soon after the turn of the year they started to build a new nest in the tree at the end of the terrace. They were voracious feeders too, stripping the cones and eating the soft bits at the base of each petal, like people eating artichokes. Every morning the litter of gnawed chips and stripped cones was there to remind us that everything was going well, and one day a squirrel dropped a nibbled cone, well aimed to hit me on the shoulder, as a further reminder that they were still with us.

By the end of February, the day temperature was breaking into the twenties, and the almonds were in full blossom. The purple irises were bursting into flower and a few little birds that knew it was safe to twitter at this time of year were beginning to do so. Spring was on the doorstep, life was awakening. The Fête of St. Baudile was only ten weeks away, and it was that which really marked for us the beginning of full summer. There might be a rare heavy rain shower during the next six months, and, like everyone else, we hoped there would be, but the event was unlikely in the extreme. Our mini-climate of this part of the

Minervois rarely put up its arms. Usually it kept the rain clouds at bay, and if they piled up to such an extent that they could overcome all resistance, they generally vented their fury elsewhere than on Montouliers. So we had to accept the unbroken drought of summer, and thanks to our fifteen outlets of Bas Rhône irrigation water, that was something we could face without regrets.

From St. Baudile onward the day temperature in the shade would seldom fall below 25° – indeed, that was a rare enough event for us to note it. And the warm weeks of probably unbroken sunshine were welcomed not just by ourselves but by the many others who shared with us our happy domaine. The siskins were flashing from tree to tree across our lawn as though giving us a farewell display before setting off for other haunts, and already the bee-eaters were twisting and fluttering from their observations posts on our telephone wire. Of all our birds these were the most beautiful, their blue and red, yellow and green plumage flashing in the brilliant sun. And there were the hoopoes.

I always admired these birds, and in earlier years we had often seen them along the banks of the Canal du Midi. They would sometimes walk sedately across our lawn, pausing to drive a long and curving beak through the turf to hit a grub and not, I hoped, one of the half bricks and pieces of tiles which always appear so mysteriously under the most carefully sown grass. Then they would look up, display their splendid crests like ladies trying on expensive hats, and move on to the next insect.

Curiously enough, it was a long time before I realised that it was the hoopoe that was responsible for the clear, clarinet-like note that I could sometimes hear when walking through the woodlands of Le Pech. It should have been obvious – after all, it was not for nothing that Linnaeus gave it the name *Upupa* – but the clear, musical, wonderfully pitched 'oop-oop-oop-oop' floating over the scrub and the vines puzzled me. I tried to copy it, and eventually succeeded in getting the bird to start a conversation with me and at last reveal itself in its dipping flight and the flash of black and white on its wings.

By the end of the month the Scops owl was calling from the bushes down in the *ruisseau du village*. For a long time I persisted in telling our visitors that it was a frog – not the Aristophanes

. . . sitting side by side like avian humpty-dumpties

variety but a small green one which lived in trees. This was not intended to deceive them. Some years earlier I had met such charming little creatures along the bank of the Canal de Brienne in Toulouse, and I had seen how the frog could blow up a huge pinkish balloon under his chin and use it as a resonator, or maybe as a Scot playing the bagpipes. The sound was beautiful, musical, and a charming addition to the otherwise man-made sounds of that mooring near the city centre, but, of course, it was less loud than the Scops call, which very much resembled one single 'oop' of the hoopoe.

The Scops was, to me, a stranger. Littler than the little owl, and shorter overall than a thrush, it looked like an Edward Lear owl, especially around the ears and nose, and I could well imagine it sailing away for a year and a day with its friend and fiancée the pussy-cat. Usually it was invisible in the tangle of the *ruisseau*, or in our olive trees, but sometimes it would be overcome by curiosity and venture to sit on a branch of the pine at the end of our terrace to watch us enjoying the fading light of evening. When I say 'it' I mean 'they', for there could be two or even three individuals sitting side by side like avian humpty-dumpties.

Snails began to appear too. The large edible snail of the French cuisine tended to hide away until after rain, but there were plenty of others. The little two-toothed turret laid a patch of babies on one of the vines, but the commonest was a small, whitish one which was so addicted to fennel that the clusters of them over the plants could make a roadside verge look as though there had been a snowstorm.

Midsummer Day brought us the oddity of a cicada which continually flew in a tight circle. It was not difficult to catch, and when I examined it the unfortunate insect was found to be suffering from a genetic, or more probably developmental, defect. One wing was only a third the size of the other, so steering was impossible. But he could zizz well enough, and continued to do so until ten minutes past ten that day, when the union order to keep quiet was flashed around the pines.

This time of year was always a treat. A Great Banded Grayling, very like a Camberwell Beauty, came to uncurl its streamer of tongue and lick out the salad dish and yoghurt bowls at lunchtime. This was one of our loveliest and commonest butterflies, but while he was busy on the remains of salad dressing, I noticed a very large grey caterpillar walking up the wall toward the woodwork of the eaves. It was curious rather than beautiful, and as soon as it was disturbed it withdrew its trunk-like proboscis. This was the first elephant hawk moth caterpillar I had seen in seventy-five years.

Nor had I ever before seen a specimen of the Death's Head hawk moth caterpillar, but this gorgeous creature of emerald green with blue and red slashes appeared on a bush at the side of the path through the *pinède* where we often took a walk after lunch. I was worried that it was too obvious and would eventually attract a bird or some other predator, but we decided not to move it but to watch it, day by day. It consumed a quantity of leaves and always seemed to me to be far too conspicuous against the more olive tone of the bush, but it survived. Eventually the time came when it was preparing to pupate, and we were happy to see it making its way little by little toward the base of the bush, to burrow into the grass and disappear.

The moth itself, perhaps the most striking of all the European moths, was something I had never seen until one day I came upon a dead one in the village street. Evidently it had collided with the windscreen of a car. But its huge body with a broad blue stripe and the startling skull shape of the design on the back of the thorax make it not only the largest but the most beautiful of all the hawkmoths. I can well imagine the excitement of Vincent van Gogh when one flew into his room in the mental hospital at St. Remy-de-Provence, and how he regretted having to kill it in order to be able to paint its portrait. But he did, and that is how we can be sure what the moth was. He did not, however, relate whether or not it squeaked when he handled it, for squeaking is an accomplishment which this species has. Maybe he slaughtered it so quickly that it had no chance to cry out.

Then, one morning, a small lizard appeared in the kitchen sink and had to be helped out. However, much stranger was when we returned late at night from a concert and found a large toad comfortably seated on the kitchen worktop. We never solved the mystery of how it got there, for the top protruded a little over all the cupboards and equipment and was installed ninety-five centimetres above the floor – the extra ten being in deference to our both being rather tall. Now a toad, whether small or large, cannot jump. Certainly it could never spring from the floor, and I doubt if even a frog could have managed such a leap. But there was no other access. And there it sat, watching us and making occasional gulps, wrinkling the skin below its chin. There was only one possibility, that, in fact, it was not really a toad at all but one of those toad-look-alikes that turn up in the legends of every country in Europe. No, not a real *Bufo bufo*, but a bewitched princess turned into amphibian form by a wicked uncle and awaiting year after year the liberation that could only come by three kisses from a gallant and intrepid suitor. Meanly, perhaps, I did not try to break the spell, but carried the young lady out to a damp and shady retreat in the drainpipe that ran under our drive.

Word must have been passed around among the insects that our terrace was a good place to play around on provided one was not an ordinary wasp or a hornet. Having lunch and supper outside, we were well placed to watch the visitors to the wall of the house, where they could enjoy the warmth, and also those to the long line of clay window-boxes which we had brought from Spain, from which pink geraniums reared in the cave cascaded over the wall to fall toward the steps. There must have been some special attraction in the nectar of these flowers, for there was never an hour of sunshine when they were not visited. The pine hawk and the convolvulus hawk moth, both moths of extreme beauty and which I had never before seen, would pay occasional visits, while the humming-bird hawk would be there all the time. It was fascinating to see how these lovely little creatures, their wings beating so fast as to make only a visual blur, would hover with their slightly curving tongues almost a body length ahead, ready to reach right down into the recesses of the flowers.

Down the steps below the geraniums were the morning glories, those most beautiful of bindweeds with large flowers of heavenly blue or episcopal purple, fresh every morning. We would count the new flowers at breakfast until the blooms reached one hundred daily, and then we gave up. And if we liked these plants, so, of course, did the convolvulus hawk-moth, another great hoverer and with such a long tongue that I managed to measure it. Two inches long, this suction tube could reach anything.

To the moths were added the butterflies, the commonest being the Great Banded Grayling, and, of course, those exquisite creatures, the Swallowtails. We had the common Swallowtail in plenty over the big oleanders, but almost as many of the 'Scarce' Swallowtails, which were not scarce at all and could at once be distinguished by the length of the twin tails.

Then there were the predators too, not birds but other insects. There was a cunning species of large wasp, more wasp-waisted than any other, which was carnivorous and would alight over a spider – a small kind of tarantula sufficiently well-established in the area to have the name *Lycosa narbonensis* – neatly imprison it within the cage of six mighty legs, paralyse it with a well-placed injection of poison from its sting, and then rise like a helicopter to carry its victim away. Another cunning little creature was the bright green and hairy crab spider which could sit invisible on a geranium leaf and suddenly dart out, walking sideways, to grab an incautious fly.

The wall furnished us with a supply of curiosities, the smaller of which were likely to fall prey either to lizards behind the flower tubs or to the scorpions always on the watch from their hiding-place behind the edge of the shutters. But the large ones were safe, and some of them were very large indeed. We had the giant longhorns – *Ergates faber* and *Monochamus galloprovincialis* – and *Saga pedo* the long and awkward-looking stick insect. Egyptian grass-hoppers sometimes sat there, and now and again a mantis, green or purple, would drop in for a few minutes of prayer.

We had occasional glow-worms, romantic at night but dull fellows when seen in the light of a torch. I have always admired them for their ability to be 96% efficient in terms of the energy put in and the light got out of their chemical reactions. Discharge-tube lamps were probably the best that humans could provide, though nowhere near as efficient, and the ordinary electric lamp bulb rarely reaches an efficiency of 6%, the remainder being lost in heat.

But everywhere throughout our domaine the summer brought out the ants. I think the ant population of our land exceeded by far the human population of Britain. We had no objection to them outside the house, but we would draw a line of chemical barrier across some of their tracks to prevent, as far as we could, their access to the kitchen; even then, some would establish a new route, and we were obliged to frustrate them by leaving food overnight in dishes on a tray flooded with a shallow pond of water. Ants are ingenious, but they cannot swim.

So we were never alone. In fact, compared with most of these delightful creatures, we were a very rare species indeed.

10

Problems Alive

Montouliers was situated in a little patch of France which enjoyed a climate utterly different from Mazamet, St. Pons, and all the other places on the further side of the watershed between the Atlantic and the Mediterranean. And that special climatic area was even further sharpened into the territory of the Minervois, where there might be no rain at all for nine months on end, apart from occasional localised thunderstorms of quite extraordinary ferocity. This region of special climate was comparatively small, and limited to a triangle which had as its three corners the cities of Carcassonne, Béziers and Narbonne. Within that area, and at the domaine of Les Cactus, the weather was utterly reliable, and any incipient clouds would be swiftly driven out to sea or vaporised by the powerful puffing of the Tramontane. This blessed wind ensured that any clouds which held water were so harried that, like bombers chased by fighter aircraft, they would lighten their load by dropping it in order to make a more speedy escape. The rain fell on the western and southern edges of the Massif Central, or on the Pyrenees, but like the plagues of Egypt it passed over us.

This meant that from March until October we could be sure of having dinner out-of-doors, and between the house and the scrub and cypress at the side of the cliff we could establish a permanent dining-room totally and reliably *al fresco*, with no awful forebodings about possible drizzle.

For much of the summer our delight in open-air dining was enhanced by the presence of the cicadas, which flew in and out of the giant umbrella pine and landed on its bark to strike up their busy rasping, a repetitive and boring mating call but one which has in it the real essence of the south. Cicadas would also sit on the wall of the house, and they often had the curious habit of flying straight at my face to fall by a mistake down the open neck of my shirt, the love song being transmuted into a sort of high speed pectoral massage. We loved the cicadas and even treasured the empty pinkish ghosts we found on the vines where, after years of solitary confinement underground, they had crept up into the daylight to clutch a vine stem and split open lengthwise, crawling out of their own skins to start immediately upon a carefree but all too brief life of sexually attractive zizzing. Attractive, that is, to other cicadas of the same species and opposite sex (for there were three species involved in providing the combined orchestration) but alluring also to us. And if one of their number, carried away in a fit of zizzing exuberance, fell on its back and remained there as though dead, we would always pick it up and launch it into the air to find a perch from which to resume its curious scissoring signal of undying affection.

Often there would be a pause at about nine-thirty, as though the insects all needed a rest. It seemed to us as though somewhere there was a great union boss of cicadas who decreed that they must not give too much value for no money. But after a while some of the bolder ones would become tired of the prohibition and would defiantly strike up again in the giant tree until the darkness began to fall in its slow and silken fashion. Then, one by one, they would give up courting and perhaps go to sleep. We often recorded the time of the last cicada song of the day, and twenty-two minutes past ten was the latest that we ever noted.

The cicadas were lovable, and they were never a nuisance except to any friends who had hearing aids and found the volume of noise too much for them. Their happy singing made them part of our summer-time family, but we had not the same affection for the hornets. I would willingly have subscribed a life-membership to a fund for providing deprived cicadas with suitable cypresses, but never to one for encouraging hornets. If we noted the time of the last cicada, we also recorded the number of hornets killed during supper.

During our first autumn it was easy enough to get rid of the insects because they had left their previous domaine on the face of the cliff, where they had lived like a colony of Anatolian hermits, and decided instead to install themselves in the top of our chimney. A big fire in the hearth, a couple of armfuls of damp pine-needles, and pouf – that was the end of the nest. A few dozen hornets flew around the roof aimlessly for the next week or two, but hornets are strangely lacking in intelligence and do not seek to attack the stranger who assaults them or destroys their nest. Wasps are different. Set fire to the entrance to a wasps' nest and you need to run, and run fast.

The hornets' next nest was back on the cliff again, and the occupants obviously thought – as far as hornets can think at all – that to travel the forty yards through the trees between the cliff and our dining area was not worth the trouble, and they left us well alone. But the following year they took up residence in the dummy chimney which also contained the siren of an alarm, an extra and genuine one installed in addition to the two ostentatious but empty boxes which I had brought from Soleil d'Oc and mounted prominently. The best way to study hornets was to open the front door for longer than the delay period in the relay, so that the siren would howl. Hornets appear to be sensitive to a shattering noise produced within inches of their city of comb, and ours would come boiling out like a swarm of bees heading for a new place to live. Again, they did not attack us, and I decided to leave them in the chimney as an extra reinforcement for the siren. Burglars were unlikely, I thought, to have much in the way of detailed comparative knowledge of the behaviour patterns of the *hymenoptera* and they would probably down tools and run. This suspicion was borne out by the discovery of a symbol chalked on the electricity switch-box up the lane by our entry, a sign which I checked against the list in the insurance office at Lézignan and found to mean '*maison dangereux – danger d'approcher*'. It was pleasant to know that the *cambrioleurs* alleged to have taken Madame Real's bedstead were now recommended by their fellows to try their luck elsewhere – probably at Soleil d'Oc.

However, we found that some of our guests reacted as badly to hornets as they did to our harmless scorpions, so when these impressive insects began to arrive at dusk to crawl around the two lamps on the wall of the terrace or alight on the plates of food, we began to attack them with the table mats. Floppy fly-swatters were useless, for the hornets were well armoured in their tough stripey casing, and a heavy smack was needed to knock one down to the ground where it could, with luck, be quickly stamped upon before it had recovered from its surprise.

We quite enjoyed this supper-time sport, but visitors were less enthusiastic and were worried about our standing on chairs to smite hornets against the stucco. Worried enough not to volunteer to help.

When, one evening, we had slaughtered fifteen at a single sitting (not that we had more than one sitting for supper) we decided reluctantly that the *frelons* – as the French call them – were winning. We knew that dealing with *frelons* was one of the duties of the fire brigade who, as we discovered in our voyaging days on the waterways of France, were also the only body authorised to take up corpses from the canal or river while the police – who had called them by radio – stood casually by to watch them tackle a not particularly pleasant task. So I drove over the hill to Bize, where there was a mighty fire-station equipped with water-tankers, pump-lorries, sometimes even a helicopter, and doubtless a set or two of boules to while away the time. I explained our problem to the duty officer.

'*Des frelons?*' He was very sympathetic. *Frelons* were a burden, even perhaps a danger. Yes, possibly a mortal danger. One should not let oneself be piqued. And we had killed fifteen at dinner? *Oh, la la!* he would see to it that those of the corps of firemen who specialised in frelon-destruction would come and deal with them. *Mais oui*, it was their pleasure, of course. *Pas de problème.* Then he asked where the hornets found themselves.

'In the burglar alarm,' I said.

He laughed. *Formidable, quoi?* That would teach any intending robbers a lesson – though not if the specialists of the *pompiers de Bize* had removed them. And where was the alarm?

'On the roof. In the chimney-stack.'

Bien. It would let itself arrange itself. And the address?

I told him. 'It is the house beside the cave.'

'Oh, la la!' He clicked his teeth then made a gesture of commiseration. 'The *frelons* are not ours. This is the *département de l'Aude.* Your house is in another *département*, l'Hérault. I am desolate, but we cannot attack a nest in the Hérault. It is not our territory.'

'*Non?*'

'*Non.*' A conflagration was one thing – I had seen the Bize *pompiers* fast asleep under a tree on the Pech, guarding against possible embers rekindling a recent blaze in the woodland. The tree was in the Hérault right enough, and that was perhaps the

Dealing with hornets was one of the
duties of the fire-brigade

reason why they were asleep. Evidently firefighters knew no abstract theoretical boundaries, whereas hornets had strictly circumscribed local affiliations.

But we could call the *pompiers* in the Hérault, of course. They would come, he said encouragingly. Every fire-brigade was competent to deal with *frelons*, or indeed any other problem. So he would commend to us a visit to the *pompiers* at Quarante.

The village of Quarante, some ten minutes from Montouliers, was not one in which we had had any business, apart from visiting the Socavi store, which stocked everything a vintner might conceivably want and where we could buy very cheaply bundles of chestnut stakes for supporting new vines, or older ones which were feeling a bit weak at the knees. The village was, of course, the subject of a local joke.

One day I was chatting to a vine-dresser of our village about the excellent view that was to be had from the walk along the plateau ridgeway.

'Yes,' he said. 'And did you know that from up there you can see forty-three villages?'

'Forty-three? I don't believe it.'

'Ah, but you can. I have counted them myself. Quarante and three others besides.'

I went to the *Mairie* at Quarante to ask where the *pompiers* lived and moved and had their being, and the heavy *chef de bureau* was kindness itself. It was not an *incendie*, it was *frelons*, yes?

In a moment our hornets were the centre of discussion by the *chef*, the girl who worked the duplicator, two men who had come to get gun-licences, and a young man who was hoping to arrange for his wedding. *Frelons?* But are they not near Bize? Yes, but Bize is in the Aude. Ah . . . Then it is the affair of Quarante. *Oui, oui,* but the *pompiers* have no material for that. Yes they do. No they don't. Remember when Madame Quelquechose came in in such a rage . . . *Oh, la la!* She was a real picture. And just because that grandson of hers had been stung by a wasp! And the *pompiers* at Quarante had no material to deal with the nest. Oh, it was a scream . . .!

We all laughed uproariously at the memory which I did not happen to share.

Yes, and the *pompiers* had to ask Capestang.

It sounded to me as though this was something of a disgrace, but no; evidently Capestang was regarded with awe.

'Ah, Capestang . . .'

Yes, Capestang should know what to do.

The *chef* picked up his phone and began a conversation in what I took to be Occitan, the *langue d'Oc.* He nodded sagely, reported our location, put down the phone and told me that Capestang would deal with the *frelons.*

That was good. When, I asked.

'An hour perhaps . . .'

An hour! I expected it to be in theory next week and in practice next month at the earliest.

'They will come when the sun is setting. Then most of the hornets will be at home. That will be the time to attack.'

We shook hands all round, and I drove home to await the sound of the march of the gladiators.

It was about half past seven when a smart, bright red and spotless car arrived, with two handsome and exuberant young men. One of them had come to zip up the other into a special suit of armour in which to attack *frelons*. With visor, gloves and boots all in one piece with the suit there was not the tiniest aperture or crevice in which a *frelon* could successfully attack him.

This done, we put our ladder up to the roof, the attendant passed up the spray cylinder and pump and insecticide, and the fighter walked carefully up the tiles, flatfooted, so as not to crack them. His companion stood at the top of the ladder to photograph him at work.

I had expected it to be a matter of a quick spray, a furious issuing of enraged insects, and that would be that. But no. The fireman sprayed the colony for nineteen minutes, and all the while the insects flew casually in and out as though nothing unusual was happening. When the entire canister of fluid had been pumped into the cavity, the man on the roof asked for a big spoon, and then carefully began to dig out the comb, throwing the chunks down to the ground. Much of it was old and discoloured, but soon he reached the newer stock and big pieces came flying through the air. I picked one or two of them up to examine them. Some of the hexagons contained large white grubs with light brown heads, others were capped over with a silky dome.

'*Bon. C'est tout!* The two firemen came down from the roof and the one who had been doing the work was unzipped. He was dripping with sweat, for it was one of the really hot days of summer and he was wearing his thick serge flame-repellent suit under his special hornet-proof armour. He took off the jacket, and a pullover too, and sat steaming off in a T-shirt. Then he selected a large piece of the comb, one which had free larvae in it and capped cells also, and took it over to the car.

'For my children. I can show them the life history of the *frelons*,' he said.

It was difficult to know just how to thank our visitors for a job well done. A *pastis*, perhaps? No, not when driving a fire-brigade car. A beer might have been permissible, but was hardly adequate. Besides, this was a wine district, and beer was more of a drink for seaside visitors, Dutchmen and the like.

Ingrid had an idea. She knew from experience that if there

was one thing that invariably went down well, and was a new taste to the French palate, that was Swedish *snaps*. We were actually out of Swedish, but we had some Aalborg which was the next best thing, and to the non-Swedish palate just as good. She fetched a bottle for them to take home for a celebration, whenever one was due.

It could not have been a better present. We parted the best of friends, and assured the young men that we would shortly be sending them the photos we had also taken of them engaged in their intrepid task.

'And any time you have *frelons* . . .' said the gladiator.

We had the feeling that he hoped we would.

Sometimes the feral life of Montouliers provided us with unexpected situations. When, one autumn, we returned after a month-long absence at the end of the *vendanges*, we encountered a curious problem with the toilet.

Our loo for visitors, *hoi poloi*, and even for ourselves if the need was urgent, opened discreetly out of the hall. The Real Consorts had only one loo, and that was in a closed box within the bathroom, but as we were not French we liked to have efficient ventilation. Yves Passet was our electrical contractor and he came from Paraza. He was the smallest man I had ever seen, and he was able to creep around between the walls and rafters in the roof space to place his cables and junction boxes where larger mortals would have failed or become stuck. It was he who installed an extractor fan in the ceiling of the toilet, and this drew out the air and voided it into the roof space itself. It was fitted with a timer and coupled to the light switch. Close the toilet door having turned on the light, and the fan would whirr away like a helicopter and continue to do so for two minutes after one's planned exit. The idea was simple and efficient. It worked.

But when, one October day, we returned and I went into our hall toilet, I turned on the light switch and nothing happened. There was, however, a cabinet over the basin, and this was fitted with a strip light. I turned it on. *Pas de problème*. Certainly not in that fitting. But one did not need to be Sherlock Holmes to deduce that if two electrical items shared a switch and neither would function it was reasonably probable that the cause lay in the switch-gear.

I did not ring Yves Passet, but took an insulated screwdriver to prise off the switch-cover. The contacts looked to me to be in good order, but maybe the tumbler was not tipping as far as it should.

So I unscrewed the whole affair from the wall and found that this was so. And what was preventing the proper function was a live and vigorous greyish larva with six legs near the front, and twelve brownish pupae like miniature bratwursts with transverse bands. I scooped them all out with care, reassembled everything in the switch-box, turned on the light and extractor, and that was that.

Except that I was puzzled. The wires came down inside the hollow bricks of the interior wall in what Jersey electricians called a 'condewit'. So this whole menagerie must have entered the switch that way too. There was no other possibility. They had come marching down the wiggly plastic piping till they could go no further. There they had taken up suitable positions and pupated – all except one, which was presumably the last arrival.

Anyhow, the light and fan worked again in a sober and orderly fashion. But not for long. Two days later the switch was reluctant to make a contact, and I took it all apart again. This time there were ten handsome grubs like the first one, and two pupae. I gathered them up and started to look at illustrations of insect larvae, but this was hardly successful because entomologists like depicting gorgeously coloured moths and butterflies but can rarely be bothered with the less glamorous earlier stages. The only grub they resembled, and very closely too, was that of the glow-worm, but I thought we could discount that in spite of Ingrid's suggestion that maybe they had entered the electrical system to charge up their batteries.

The next thing was to take a lamp and creep around the roof space to see how these fascinating denizens had got into the conduit.

I located the pipe from the toilet and followed it. Soon there was a junction box, but that branch went to the extractor. I followed the main line, which went to another junction box. Pursuing each branch I came to more junctions, until one line descended to the fuse box, totally enclosed in a cupboard downstairs. There was not a single place where the piping was broken, or fell short of its objective. It was a closed system.

But that was not possible. There was, I realised, on either

side of the house a heat-sensitive automatic lamp which I had myself installed on the flat boarding under the eaves. They were very sensitive indeed and were occasionally set off by a squirrel or a visiting cat, and they surprised poor Étienne when he went to check the house in his capacity as *guardien* during our absence. He was just walking up the drive when the light came on. Courageously, he ran round to the back of the house to tackle any intruder – and the light went off. He raced back to the front. Not a soul in sight, so he tiptoed round the corner. The light came on again. He told me later he had been thoroughly scared by the mystery.

The wires to these lamps were also in conduits which I had laid myself, as I did not like the idea of wires being stapled along wooden beams. They were totally enclosed all the way from new junction boxes to the exterior, where they passed out through the woodwork into each lamp. If a creature could creep through the quarter-inch hole beside the wires it might conceivably get into the piping and, unable to turn around, march onward from junction box to junction box until it reached the end at a switch.

Next day the switch worked perfectly but when the light was turned on a grub fell out of the fan. I gathered it up and took my specimens down to the Department of Health and Environment in Narbonne. I had been there once before when a visitor suffered some mosquito bites and I wanted to know how to proceed to get rid of those noxious insects.

'Ah. You say this happened at Montouliers?'

'Yes. Last night, and . . .'

'There are no mosquitoes at Montouliers.'

'But . . .'

'There are *no* mosquitoes at Montouliers. And anyway, it is in the Hérault.'

Interdepartmental trouble again, I could see.

'Well,' I said, 'suppose we are bitten at Bize.' That was in the Aude all right.

The official looked thoughtful. 'But you were not. If you were to live in Bize you might be bitten, *bien sur*. However . . .'

'There are no mosquitoes at Montouliers,' I got in first. 'Many thanks for your help.'

However, if any visitors later told us they had been bitten, I now had it on official authority that they must be mistaken. I

141

stuck to this line, and, oddly enough, I believe it was true. No mosquito has ever annoyed me. Not in Montouliers.

On this later occasion there were two men and a woman chatting about some weighty concern of public *santé*. After a while I coughed discreetly.

'*Monsieur?*'

We shook hands. I took out my tame grub and let it walk over my palm.

'Well?'

The environmental officer looked at it. 'A *chenille*.'

'Yes, I know it's a sort of caterpillar, but what sort?'

'Hm.' The others had a look too. They confirmed that it was a grub. A caterpillar. But what of it?'

'I want to know if it is harmful?'

'How can it be harmful?'

'Well, if these grubs crawl out of the electric fittings . . . I thought maybe . . .'

'The electrical fittings?'

'Yes. The light on the toilet would not switch on, and I found the *interrupteur* to be full of insect grubs. I removed them, and the next day there were more. Then they appeared in the ceiling light. Then next day in the lamp on the shaving mirror . . .'

'Yes?'

'Yes, they seem to creep along the wires, somehow.'

'Very interesting . . .' I detected a wink across one of the desks. I could see that I was being regarded as a lunatic, but probably harmless. Nobody was telephoning for a straight-jacket. Not yet.

'They must come down the plastic conduits.'

'Of course.' A reassuring smile.

'But where from?' I persevered. Looks were exchanged, but I noted that everyone present had a fixed smile. Evidently I was not regarded as dangerous, provided one made no sudden movements or noises. Keep him at ease, that was the thing. Avoid anything that could cause hysteria. I wondered if anyone was going to get a message to the medical officer, but I could not detect anybody writing a hurriedly scribbled note asking for help.

'How do they get into the electric system?' I pressed the point.

'From outside it,' the woman said, with a winning smile.

'Quite. But if they get into the conduits they must come from somewhere. Would they bore into the roof timbers?'

'*Ah non, ah non.*'

'Well, *what are they?*'

'You should ask the Department of Forests.' The official looked up a telephone number. The office was about forty miles away. 'If you have pine-trees, they are probably pine-tree insects.'

'You mean pine weevils? Like *Tomicus piniperda?*' That was an excellent piece of one-upmanship.

'Maybe.'

'But *Tomicus* grubs are smaller.' I knew this from identifying half a century earlier the borers in the pine plantation at Ainsdale, where the family had a summer cottage.

'Yes?'

'Yes. Well, thank you for your help.'

'*C'est rien.*' That was true enough.

'You have a pine near the house?' It was the official who had not yet spoken. I think he wanted to make sure I would depart contented.

'Yes. An enormous *pin parasol*. Fifteen or twenty metres high.'

A tongue click. 'They perhaps drop off it and blow under the tiles.'

'And go straight for the electric system?'

'So it seems.'

I put my exhibit back in its jar. I sensed that the interview was not going to get anywhere. But I would have a last try.

'Can you suggest any remedy?'

'Treat the tree, of course.'

'And how do I do that?'

'It is not for us to say. You should ask the Forestry Department. *Au revoir, et bonne journée!*'

So that was the end of the matter. But not for long. Two days later I found a couple of the grubs walking along the floor in the hall. Then more appeared in the shaving lamp over the basin, and again in the ceiling bowl. And after an absence of four days we came back to find the toilet switch needed emptying yet again. I did not go back to Narbonne with our problem, but I despatched two little packets of live grubs, one to a friend in

Yorkshire who had contact with the world of arboriculture, the other to a friend in Cambridge, and it was from the Zoological laboratory there that the riddle was solved – at least in part.

One of the insects had the good fortune to hatch out from the small brown pupa case, and no doubt it was astonished to find itself the object of scrutiny in that great centre of learning. Another emerged in the jam-pot on my desk in Montouliers during our next absence. These flies were handsome creatures with three gold stripes down the thorax and two large golden spots on the abdomen, and they were identified in Cambridge as one of the *Stratiomyidae* (Soldier flies) and of a species not known in Britain.

The larger grubs, the greyish ones with a flattened body and six anterior legs, were temporarily named by me *Enigma electroconduiti Pilk*, pending more exact identification. In the end they turned out indeed to be a species of pine weevil, not the *Tomicus piniperda* of my youth but a larger one, *Hylobius abietis*. So far so good, but to this day we have not discovered how they get into the electrics, although we can always be sure that if we return after a few weeks of absence they will be there to greet us, crawling round the bowl of the light or interfering with the switch in the toilet.

11

Hunters All

Every year in the autumn the season of hunting – that is, shooting – would begin. I was well aware that this was as much of a tradition in France as Father Christmas was in England, but I did not like it. Anything that moved was liable to be shot at, and even if lark's tongues were not quite so highly prized as once they were, I wondered if that might not simply be because the soaring songsters had been shot almost to extinction. The most noticeable thing about French woodland was the total absence of birdsong. Maybe natural selection was ensuring that only birds with defective vocal cords survived. The warbler that dared to warble had better migrate in time or it would be shot on sight – though, fortunately, to sight a warbler at all was no easy matter.

Anyone living in France but not of French origin is bound to wonder at *la Chasse*, and to ponder why it is such an obsession. Some would go so far as to say that it represents a national streak of cruelty and violence well illustrated by Napoleon (now somewhat disowned in that country), and that the Frenchman is by nature blood-thirsty. Personally, I do not think this is so. The French obsession with shooting is in no way like the upper-crust hunting-and-shooting and pheasant-raising tendency of what is left of the English aristocracy, but seems to be merely the counterpart of the equally bizarre if slightly less dangerous English obsession with angling.

There are, of course, anglers in France (and plenty of them), along the rivers and canals, but it is not the same at all. They tend (with a few exceptions, such as the one that once assaulted me for passing by in a boat) to be contented and sunny individuals. They like to sit in pleasant scenery in the company of a friend perhaps, and a bottle of wine or maybe two, and while away part of the afternoon amid scenery which has inspired some of the greatest painters. It is not the same occupation at all as fishing in an English canal.

Any Frenchman, whether angler or not, would be astonished if he saw the English angling fraternity about their serious occupation, and he might wonder that anybody could spend the day so dismally, sitting in the drizzle with no other objective than to catch something useless and inedible and then return it to the water. The French fisherman takes home and eats what he catches – however unspeakable the object. The English angler angles for angling's sake, and in this way he is, I think, like the French *chasseur*. Both of the armies, piscatorial and *chasseur*, are fanatically dedicated to something which is traditional and perhaps has an element of bravado in it; but at least it can be said of *la Chasse* that it occasionally (if rarely) yields something for the table. So I think it is not a sign of any particularly vicious trait in the French character. But I am sorry for the birds, just the same. When shot, they cannot be put back into the air, as fish can into the canal.

Our first encounter with *la Chasse* was at Soleil d'Oc. One Sunday morning at the opening of the season I looked out of the kitchen window and saw three not very attractive men with guns strolling across our premises. They were dressed in leftovers from the American army stores, and looked like the tail end of the retreat from Moscow. I went out to them. What were they doing, I asked.

'*C'est la Chasse . . .*'

Not here, I said.

But they had always shot over this heath. Always. It was *la Chasse*.

'Maybe it was,' I said. 'But no longer. This territory is sanctuary for birds. And for rabbits,' I added. 'Clear out of here.'

The men groused and grumbled a bit, but I insisted. Nobody was going to slaughter songsters in my garden, I said. I would protect them, and nobody would come over that land shooting without asking me first, and then I would refuse.

The *chasseurs* sauntered on, and entered next the de Kaases area. I told them it was private and they had better clear off. I followed them to the van der Borns. They too were absent at this time of year, and I was not at all certain that the alleged *chasse* might not be a cover for a bit of housebreaking, as the men appeared a very unsavoury trio. But then, to some extent, *chasseurs* were bound to look suspicious if they appeared in such drab and bedraggled get-up.

Like other villages, Montouliers was dedicated to *la Chasse* when the season opened. Our friend M. Fabre, the ironmonger in the neighbouring village of Argeliers, had his window filled with guns and other equipment and did a brisk trade in cartridges. When walking on the *garrigue* or at the edge of the woodlands I would often come upon a scatter of empty shotgun cartridges, not just one or two but as many as fifty or sixty at a single station. That represented a lot of blazing away, and if even the lovely red-legged partridges, always in groups and so slow to take off, had survived in such numbers in the area, the only explanation I could think of was a certain inaccuracy of aim which might not perhaps have passed a breathalyser test.

The occasional pot-shot at a bird or a rabbit flushed from the vines was probably as much as most *chasseurs* could accomplish. And the economics puzzled me. So much equipment and so little visible result, and in some village houses a rack holding enough firearms (and expensive ones too), to make one think a terrorist cache had been discovered by the *gendarmerie*. But, of course, most of this was for use with the real big game, the wild boar.

Such hunting required dogs. Monsieur Real had had his compound for hunting dogs, and they existed all through the village. They were mostly a mixture of a kind of spaniel and something like a setter; pleasant, amiable fellows, full of curiosity, and usually living in a chicken-run. Étienne had dogs, his family had dogs, M. Jaumot had four or five. That was in no way unusual. All these animals had to be fed, regardless of cost, and it was no surprise to us to see that whole sections of a supermarket would be devoted to dog food, nor that near Mazamet there was a factory for doggy meals. Investing in the manufacture of dog food would, I thought, be a good hedge in a depression. The French *chasseur* would go short himself, or at least let his wife go short, rather than cut the canine rations, I realised.

The dogs had also to be transported to the scene of the hunt. Generally, this meant having an old car available, but very often a man would have a Renault Quatre van, specially

Dogs existed
all through the
village

equipped. None of these basic requirements could be provided on peanuts, but, miraculously enough, it seemed that they could indeed be carried on *vin de table* production – another item of which the economics were beyond my understanding.

I was never very impressed by the intelligence of the spanielly *chiens de chasse*. These dogs lay about in the village street, so lazy that one had sometimes to haul them out of the roadway in order to drive past. Mental acuity was not one of their most obvious qualities, even if equanimity was. One day I was walking on a vineyard track when a little van came bumping toward me. The driver was almost frantic with worry. Had I seen three dogs? No? *Oh la la*, it was now the third day that he was hunting for them. He had driven out of the village with the dogs in the van and only just up there at the woodland he had opened the door to let them have a bit of air and pftt! One of them must have scented a rabbit. They had rushed into the wood, all three. He had shouted and called, but no dog came back.

'But surely they would come home,' I suggested. The place where he had let them out of his van was not half a kilometre from the village. 'They must know their way around.'

'No, no. They have never been outside the house except in the van. They would have no idea which way to go.' He began to shout and call, but still no dogs appeared.

'And they are good dogs,' he said, almost in tears. 'They are clever dogs, well trained.'

It hardly sounded that way, but I did not say so. I had known a not particularly bright dog in Lancashire that found its way home across twenty-five miles of totally unfamiliar country after it had been sold but evidently preferred its former owner's domaine. I commiserated with the poor man and left him to his desperate *chasse aux chiens*.

One morning I was driving to Argeliers for bread when I saw something curious in the vineyard, some twenty yards from the road. Across the ditch there was a patch where, for several rows, the vines had been smashed down, their stakes broken, and beyond that was a car lying on its roof, its wheels in the air. I noticed that all the tyres were bare of any tread, so to skid at high speed at the bend in the road would not have been difficult. I looked to make sure that there was nobody dead or injured and drove on.

The car was there for a few days. I asked in the village if anyone knew who it belonged to.

Ah yes! The car belonged to the young man who had just come as a tenant in the Clavel house. The premises had once been a bistro and it had been up for sale for two or three years, but there were no buyers. Village people did not want it, because they all wished for something more modern and convenient such as one saw on the television, so the family had to let it out as and when they could. I was sorry for the Clavels and their inability to sell, but it was understandable; people from the outside world were eccentric enough to want plumbing, and a kitchen worthy of the name.

'How did it happen?' I enquired.

I was told that, well, the young man happened to be driving along the road at two o'clock in the morning when – well, was it not extraordinary? All of a sudden three wild boar rushed across the road in front of him. He braked, and the car swerved.

'Of course,' I said. 'Were they *sangliers roses*? Pink ones?'

'*Non, non, non, non, non.* He saw them distinctly.'

I believed that, under certain circumstances, one might see pink wild boar quite distinctly too.

149

☆ ☆ ☆

After we had been a month or two at Les Cactus, I thought it might be a happy idea to provide our own visitors and others with a number of round walks, trails which would make a circuit through the wonderful countryside but would avoid, as far as possible, such few minor roads as there were. They made use of *chemins* of the foresters, vineyard tracks and small lanes, and the problem was to find cross links from one existing walkable path to another. The same problem seemed also to have occurred to rabbits, and perhaps to *sangliers*, pink or otherwise, for I could always be sure that an afternoon of searching would result in the discovery of an animal track which then only needed to be enlarged with the vine-clippers to bring it up to human standards. Having established the circuits, all of which started at the electric pole outside our entrance, I marked them with the assistance sometimes of any volunteer visiting members of our family who might enjoy the work with the paint pot. Our marking was the standard French system of one dash for 'this way', a double mark for 'change of direction' and X for 'wrong way'. Once the paths were established they were kept sufficiently trodden and open by visiting ramblers, or *promenade à cheval* riders from the pony hirers at Bize, and, of course, by animals.

The rounds varied in length from little more than one hour (the Red Earth circuit, marked in blue) to the Agel valley, a steep walk of about four hours, marked in pink, and the *Bout du Monde* round, rather longer and with marks in red. I never discovered how that particular area near Villepassans came by its name, but maybe it just reflected the ideas of an earlier generation whose horizons were even more restricted than those of the local people today.

A fact which surprised me was that when following our trails, I sometimes found that stones marked with the coloured dashes of paint had been turned over. At first I thought this was the work of children; then the idea occurred to me that perhaps somebody was snaring rabbits and did not like the small tracks on the *garrigue* to be used by humans, as the scent might put the rabbits off. I always turned the stones back again, but it was only after two years that I made the discovery of how the removal of the marks was brought about.

One day I had occasion to visit the Babeaus, who lived in a very presentable house in the village and did not have the living-room cluttered with a giant television.

'Somebody told me it was you who painted marks on the stones,' said Madame Babeau. 'Is that true?'

I said that it was. I had marked altogether six paths in different colours.

'Well, it was I who turned over the stones. I like so much to walk in the country – and I didn't want anyone else to know some of those trails. So I covered up the marks!'

We had a good laugh over it, and I gave her a map of all the paths so far marked out, and promised that we should do some of the walks together in the coming summer. I would take the paintpot, and she could take the clippers. And I assured her that she need not worry about others following the paths. The kind of people we both wanted to discourage would not take a walk of even a quarter of a mile if they were paid to.

It was pleasant soon to discover that the trails were being used, and were not just established for my own enjoyment and that of our numerous visitors. Indeed, we acquired new friends among the few from elsewhere who had discovered the marks by accident – as, for example, where a trail crossed a road on which they happened to be driving. One could assume, I thought, that anyone inclined to take a walk of an hour or two would be a sensible person and not inclined to vandalism, but then one day when I took the orange walk myself I had a shock.

This, the Lime Kiln round, gave on the return leg the most striking view of the village that was to be had from anywhere. Montouliers, cramped beneath the mass of the old chateau-fort and the curious sun-hatted tower of St. Baudile's, was a delight from whichever angle it was approached, but crossing over the top of a rough hill of prickly shrub and lavender on the orange walk one came quite suddenly upon this breath-taking view of the village against a backdrop of woodland and vineyards fading away to the horizon. And just to add an extra touch, the place where one was brought to a halt by so much beauty was carpeted with a few square yards of *Iris chamaeris*, its glorious purple flowers on stems only three or four inches high and therefore quite capable of smiling openly even when the Tramontane was trying to beat its earlier record. On this

151

particular occasion I was brought to a halt, horrified. Not a flower, or leaf, or tuber of the iris was to be seen.

Angry and saddened, I went that evening to the *Mairie*. Someone, I said, had vandalised the irises, and on ground belonging to the village too. The entire patch had gone, tubers and all. They had been ruthlessly dug up. *Iris chamaeris* was a nationally protected plant and to destroy it like this could be a serious offence. Who could have done such a thing? Trippers? Hardly, because the site was too far from a road, and anyway we were mercifully free from their visitations. There was nothing in the surroundings to attract that kind of destroyer. I was furious, not, of course, with the mayor, but at the wicked and thoughtless vandalism that had grubbed out the plants.

Monsieur Fraisse was obviously baffled. I thought he had probably never heard of *Iris chamaeris* or of the regulations defining certain species as endangered. He looked across the desk at Claudette, Claudette looked at me, and I looked at the mayor.

'I am not sure that it is our land,' he said. 'But it would not be anyone from the village.'

We went through to the library, where a plaster bust of Marianne stared across at a dusty glass-fronted bookcase which contained enough volumes of laws and regulations to cover, I thought, the whole period from the governorship of Mark Antony in Narbonne to the present day. A folder of large-scale maps was spread out on a table, and we turned them over. I was able to pinpoint the exact spot where the irises were. Or were no longer.

The mayor considered. What could he do? Here was this amiable eccentric who had come to live half the time in the village, and who clearly loved the place so much that his face was red with anger at the disappearance of some allegedly precious weed, but what, as mayor, could he do about it? And how could he protect plants a mile away on the *garrigue*? He had weightier matters to attend to, such as the rating returns and the village share of the *taxe d'habitation*, to say nothing of spraying his vines. He did not say all this, for he was far too polite, but I could read such thoughts behind his heavy eyebrows. He thanked me and we shook hands. '*Allez, et bonne soirée.*'

One day during the early spring of the following year the

152

A plaster bust
of Marianne
stared across the
library

hanging bell on the outside of the house was rung, and getting up from my lunch I was surprised to find a delegation of six standing in the drive. They had small knapsacks and mountain boots, and plenty of smiles. They were from the Ramblers Society of Marseillette, their leader told me. (Marseillette was a village near Carcassonne.) They were disturbing me?

'Not in the least,' I said.

Well, they had just had their picnic lunch, and had left another dozen of the party up at the church. They had followed the yellow marks from near Bize and had found themselves here in Montouliers. It was a beautiful walk, and very well marked, he said. And now they wanted to return to Bize by the Agel valley, over the back of the hills, but they could not find the way. Somebody in the village had said that they must ask

153

Monsieur Pilkington. He had done all the markings and he would be able to tell them which way to go. So here they were.

'One moment,' I said. 'Let me put my boots on, and I will come with you the whole way. *Bien sur.*'

It was an excellent afternoon for a walk, and I found the leader of the party to be a good naturalist and very observant. There was little he did not know, except how to find the links which led between the rocks and down the scarp to the valley of Agel. I had not actually completed all the markings of this trail, but I knew it well enough, and the party of walkers considered it one of the best outings they had had. We were approaching the peach orchards near the river, when my companion pointed to the ground.

'*Sanglier.*' Sure enough, there were pig footmarks in the mud. Perhaps there had been the remains of leftover windfalls of the jam peaches to be rootled for.

'And here. You can see the marks of the tusks where he has been digging up roots.'

So there really were real wild boar around, and not only the pink variety that overturned cars. And, of course, they would eat almost anything.

We came out of the woodland close to a farm. The lane was edged with the same tall bluish-purple irises of which we had thousands along our boundaries at Les Cactus. Some of them had been grubbed out and left in an untidy mess. I could see for myself the cloven footmarks.

'Irises,' said my companion. 'Yes. They are a favourite for *sangliers.*'

So, could that be the explanation of the vandalism? Next day I went up to the top of the orange round again, wondering if I could perhaps detect traces of pig feet so many months later. I walked quickly up the path to the corner where the irises had been. There were no piggy footmarks visible. But all around me the patches of deep purple showed where the *Iris chamaeris* was getting ready to burst into its gorgeous display. The *sangliers* had grubbed the tubers out, *bien sur*, but only the ones right on the surface.

Up until then I had privately believed that the only wild boar in the immediate neighbourhood were the pink variety. When I expressed such doubts to Étienne he seemed very taken aback. There were plenty of *sangliers*, he said. They would run down from the woods on Le Pech and raid the vineyards or anything else that might be available, he assured me. If that were so, I wondered why he and his companions went to the trouble of mounting the expeditions the way they did instead of hunting the creatures in the much easier and open country nearby, and the sparse broken woodland of Le Pech.

From time to time Étienne would announce that he was off on the following day on an expedition of *la Chasse*. Usually it was to the almost impenetrable forests of scrub oak and thorn bushes in the neighbourhood of St. Jean-de-Minervois (where an excellent muscat was also to be found). The object was declared to be wild boar, but only once in four years was he able to present us with a tasty little piece of the strong meat, and I was fairly sure that this was the only *sanglier* he and his friends ever hit.

We would sometimes see him ready to depart with a dog, and with a litre of red co-op *ordinaire* under each arm. Presumably his pals had the same equipment. They would drive in their vans over to some remote spot at the edge of impenetrable prickly scrub and the hunt would begin. The dogs might or might not find a scent, but it mattered very little. A *sanglier* could easily sort out a dog or two if they came too close, and he was much more at home in that terrain than they were. I doubted if the dogs often got a sight of their prey. Certainly, the hunters did not. The thick, prickly undergrowth was impassable. It was better to give up, relax with the wine, wait for the dogs, and then drive erratically home after a very pleasant and wine-flavoured outing.

Of course, *sangliers* were worth the hunting, even if the chase was more theoretical than practical. They could be massive beasts, with enough meat to feed the family for a month or two. But although some of the men of Montouliers were deeply involved in hunting the boar, the piece of meat Étienne gave us was the only piece I ever saw in the village.

I suspected that Étienne himself began to wonder about the alleged omnipresence of wild boar in the hilly area near St. Jean, for on the first day of January he proudly announced that he and companions and a car-load or two of dogs were off to hunt *sangliers*, as this was the last permitted day. And off they went, a miniature armoured column.

155

Next morning when Étienne arrived to continue pruning the vines I asked him how it went.

'Excellently,' he said.

'And did you get a *sanglier*?'

Well no, they didn't. Because it was a lovely sunny day (in fact 16 degrees in the shade on our thermometer) and when they reached their chosen hunting ground it was all so beautiful, and sunny, and balmy, and just such a New Year's Day as one could hardly dream of, that they decided it was very much better to sit around under a big oak tree and have a really good lunch. And a pal from Cazoules had brought a *confit de canard*. Mmmm. Wonderful. The best *confit de canard* he had had in all his life. Such a *confit* as one cannot find, no, not in the best restaurants. So they had sat around, and had *confit de canard*, and wine. Yes, they had taken plenty of wine, and that was good. And noon had passed, and the afternoon, and they had sat round just enjoying themselves until it was time to come home because dusk was falling on this last day of *chasse* for the season.

I admired that. It seemed to me a much more sensible way of spending a fine winter's day. Besides, I wanted the *sangliers* to have a happy new year too – though I doubt that they would have been in much danger if they had walked straight past the luncheon party.

All the year round we would go for a walk after lunch, except on those rare occasions when there was a downpour. Little by little we came to know the lanes and tracks over an area of several miles around, and I was continually trying to discover more links between the valleys so that I could plan out another round walk for the benefit of visitors or our friends from other villages who liked to explore. I had already marked several rounds with paint of different colours, and as we had once explored some way up a woodland track from the Défile de Marie Coquette I decided to go further in that direction and see where the path led to.

I do not know who Marie Coquette may have been, but it may have been her romantic name that led me one chilly afternoon near the end of January to set out along the forest path in a northerly direction. After half an hour or so I came to another track, which began to wind slowly up the hillside to the left. A few minutes along this path I came upon a rather

156

wrinkled individual cutting some branches of juniper with a bone-handled knife. He seemed startled as he heard a branch crack under my feet, and he stared at me.

He was short in stature, and looked for all the world more like a troll than a Languedocian, I thought, even if most of the local inhabitants were rather on the short side. But were there trolls in France? I was uncertain. I knew the French had *lutins* and I rather suspected that these too were trolls or an allied species, but I had never actually seen a *lutin* any more than I had seen a troll. Of course, Ingrid would have known what a troll was like, because they had plenty of them in the forests around her family home in Värmland; and the Värmlännings knew all about them and regularly met them if walking through the woods at night after a glass or two of *akvavit*.

The individual I now saw cutting a branch of juniper was exactly as a troll had been described to me. He had just the right bulbous nose, and rather straggly hair protruding from under the edge of his woollen cap. I knew that it was important to be gentle, and confidently friendly but not too inquisitive, so I took off my own woollen cap and gave a slight bow as I wished him a *Bonjour*.

The troll, or *lutin*, was obviously startled to see anyone in the forest, but he nodded and then gave a curious whistle through his fingers. He repeated the call a couple of times, and soon two amiable dogs came bounding exuberantly through the undergrowth to jump and try to lick my face.

'They are my young pair,' he said. 'I bring them up here every afternoon. Then I take them home. And in the evening I bring up the older ones. Every day.'

'Do they never get caught in a trap?' I asked.

'Trap?'

'Yes. All through the woods there are notices about Beware of the Traps.'

'Ah!' He laughed. 'Those are my traps. The dogs never get caught in them.'

'Are they for rabbits?'

'*Non-non-non-non*. Certainly not. They are for those that might attack the rabbits. Foxes. They come after my rabbits, and I set traps for them. There are foxes everywhere.'

'I see. And do you often catch a fox?'

He shook his head. 'No. But the traps keep them away.'

157

It sounded as though the foxes could read the notices about being aware, but I did not ask. 'What about the rabbits? Do you trap them?'

'No!' The troll beckoned me to follow him through the undergrowth, the dogs trotting beside us. Soon we came to a high fence of wire netting which surrounded an enclosure which was teeming with rabbits; white, brown, blotchy, or just rabbit-coloured. He threw the juniper twigs over the netting, and some of the animals began to nibble at them.

He beckoned to me again, and led on. Hidden in the bushes a little way off was a curious sort of shelter built of pine-branches and with a few pieces of board which might have come from the Cruzy village dump not far away on the further side of the main valley. I had to duck to follow him inside, where he pointed out with pride the old car seats arranged as a sofa and chairs, and a table which might have once been a sewing-machine.

The troll looked at me appealingly, evidently expecting some comment.

'It's a fine house,' I said. 'You must be very proud of it.'

'Yes! And all the forest is my domaine.' He waved his arm in a circle.

I could easily believe it. I had learned in Sweden that trolls usually had large territories, and were very possessive.

'I can have peace and quiet here,' he went on. 'And sometimes we have a family dinner. We can cook rabbit.' He showed me the half circle of stones which held some ashes. 'Yes, it's quiet here just now, but later, in the summer, the forest is full of evil people. Wicked people. They come here, swarming through the woods to steal my mushrooms. It is a good forest for mushrooms, but I have to be very quick to pick them before the wicked men and women come to smash and steal everything. It is terrible.'

I felt sorry for him. 'Do they steal the rabbits too?'

No, no. They cannot. You see, I keep the rabbits here until after February first. Next week. That is when the *Chasse aux Lapins* has to stop. Then I open the gate, and away they go, out into the forest, to live free. They are happy there.'

'But surely they don't come back?'

'*Bien sur* they do. One or two days before the *Chasse* begins again they come back. I feed them on meal, and old *baguettes*, and juniper. And I guard them, and the older dogs take over the watch at night.'

I thought he had arranged things very well. Rabbit with mushroom sauce would perhaps not appeal to me, but then I was always pernicketty about rabbit. I asked him what he did with the skins. Did he sell them?

He shook his head as though it was a shocking suggestion, so I did not pursue the matter any further. It was easy to change the subject, because from far away the sound of a tolling bell was carried on the still air. It was the Angelus bell, probably in Cruzy.

'Listen,' I said. 'How well the sound carries in the crisp air. Isn't it beautiful?'

He gave me a curious, disapproving look and seemed about to speak. But instead he frowned. It was as though I had said something improper, so I changed the subject again and asked him where the track led. I wanted to reach the valley again, I said, somewhere near Sainte Foi, which was a ruined farm and chapel near the end of the Marie Close gorge.

'The forest is mine,' he said gruffly. 'Mine! It all belongs to me. None is allowed to come in here. Nobody. But . . . Yes, I can tell you the way you should go.'

He told me to follow the path to the end of the fire-break, then aim for a large heap of stones. Soon I would come to a lane, he said, which went to Villepassans. When I came to a track descending to the left I was to take it. That would be the right one for me.

I thanked the owner of the forest, who merely nodded, took his knife again, and walked away without another word to resume his cutting of juniper twigs. I began to follow his directions.

The fire-break ended at the foot of a steep, rough, and extremely prickly area of rock and brambles and thorn bushes. I could see at least a dozen large heaps of stones ahead, but I persevered until I saw a pair of Dutch caravans, deserted for the winter. Each had a little formal garden with miniature terraces, and steps, and neat lines of white-painted stones. I realised that they could only be there if there was some sort of lane, and very soon I reached it. The lane aimed directly for the village about a mile ahead, and sure enough there was a branch to the left.

159

I had a map in my pocket, so I checked my position, but I could see no trace on it of a *chemin* leading down toward Sainte Foi. However, the path was broad, so I began the gentle descent. After ten minutes or so the track narrowed to become a footpath. Then it became a rabbit-track. After more than half an hour it petered out entirely in a wilderness of scrub and bramble, a thick and prickly jungle.

By this time it was a case of returning were as tedious as go o'er. Besides, it would soon be dark. I decided to go on. I was on the side of a hill, and not very far above the bed of a stream. If I could only break through to that, I would have no more trouble. The stream was bound to reach the Sainte Foi valley. I had only to walk down its bed and – *voilà! pas de problème.*

I was mistaken about the absence of any problem; there were problems more than ever. The stream was running downhill right enough, but it was continually straddled by fallen trees swathed in extremely tough creepers. The water ran over little falls from pool to pool, and because of the recent rain it was the colour of *café-au-lait* and completely opaque. I had to climb over tree-trunks, branches, and rocks and step into each succeeding pool which might – as I very soon discovered – be anything from three inches to three feet deep. Sometimes the water was over my waist. It was decidedly cold, too.

After an hour of struggling through the jungle I saw the thin branch of a vine protruding over the edge of the ravine above me. Vines! A vineyard! Vineyards always had tracks of access. I could escape!

And so I did. I hauled myself up the cliff and found that I was in a well-pruned vineyard. I stumbled through the vines to the access lane and hurried along it. Soon I could see a bluff crag close to Marie Coquette, and I knew where I was.

Eventually I reached home and warmed up in a hot bath. But I was convinced that the *lutin* or troll had given me wrong directions on purpose. Why?

Over tea I described my adventure to Ingrid. I told her about the rabbits, and the shack, and the evildoers who came in the summer and stole and smashed everything.

'And you were always kind and polite?'

'Certainly. I know very well you must not offend trolls. We got on very well. Then suddenly he seemed to cool off, just as we were chatting together. I was just saying how lovely it was to hear the Angelus bell at Cruzy, and . . .'

Ingrid shook her head. 'Didn't you know that the one thing that trolls cannot abide is a church bell? And you said it was a lovely sound! No wonder he gave you false directions.'

12

The Fixits

When we first arrived in the village we were, very naturally, strange birds, enigmas. It was not until Ingrid drew a winning ticket in the tombola that anyone knew our name, unless they happened to take a walk down the *chemin* between our two vineyards, where a name board proclaimed our identity for all to see. (Experience had taught me many years earlier that foreigners were more likely to remember a name if they actually saw it in front of them, rather than having to try to memorise it.) But as soon as we could be identified by our own name, contacts increased. The first was when a deputation of three of the village ladies, Madame Meunier, Madame Rouanet (Claudette's mother-in-law) and Madame Audirac came to the house one morning to say that there was to be an exhibition of the history of Montouliers, and they wanted also to be able to exhibit the work of local artists. This was not a question of books, but of paintings, because many people had observed me sitting in vineyards or on the towpath of the canal, trying to produce a watercolour. At that time, I had more than a dozen reasonably presentable ones hanging in Les Cactus, and I was very willing to lend them for a few weeks in the summer.

Not long afterwards, the village had a problem. The year was the bicentenary of the French Revolution, and that was an occasion that could not be allowed to pass unnoticed, even if people were not always very sure just what was being celebrated, or how it should be commemorated. The fact was that few of the French, especially in areas such as the Languedoc, were anxious to be reminded that according to French official estimates rather more than six hundred thousand citizens had been done to death by their fellows, often in the most cruel and horrible ways. Nor was Napoleon an

162

A small red-white-and-blue shield appeared on the wall of the Mairie

object of pride. A conceited, jumped-up Corsican, a Hitler born before his time who laid waste vast tracts of Europe – that was how people now frankly described the man.

The French post office had produced some innocuous special stamps, certainly. And the president was to preside over an impressive display of disciplined marching and drumming in the Champs Elysées, but something had to be done locally. In Montouliers a small red-white-and-blue shield appeared unobstrusively on the outside wall of the *Mairie*, and a handsome copy of a contemporary table of the Rights of Man was acquired by the *Mairie* and was to be displayed in the exhibition.

'It is at least something of which we in France can be proud,' said the mayor.

'Why?' I asked. 'You mean because it was drawn up by an Englishman and revised by an American?'

I doubt if that was generally known. It was probably assumed that I was joking. But the real question was how this really rather beautiful work of art was to be hung. It could not just be put up with a couple of drawing pins (*il y a des voleurs partout*, and even my watercolours were hung so high up the walls as to be out of reach, and certainly out of vision). No, it would have to be framed. But who could advise on framing an object of such size? They had better consult Monsieur Pilkington-Fixit.

163

So there was a deputation about the matter. Had I any notion of where they could find a framer who could undertake this great task?

Indeed I had. We were soon going to Jersey. Give us the *Droits de l'Homme*, and in plenty of time for the Fourteenth of July it would be brought back, framed and all. We were coming back with a loaded Volvo, and I knew it would not be too large to lie on top of the load.

Then there was the matter of colour. We tried a few tints from my painting-box and decided in the end that a darkish olive-green background showed off the silk best of all. Then we had to think about which size border would look best; and the colour of the actual frame. All these matters were gone into at great length, and a few days later we left for Jersey, where I found a suitable moulding at the timber yard, got a piece of quarter-inch ply half the size of a door, made up a properly mitred frame myself, had a non-reflecting glass cut to size, and painted the ply and the frame in the required colours, adding also hanging rings stout enough to take the weight.

This was really a very simple task, but when we came back and delivered the framed Rights of Man to the *Salle des Expositions*, everyone seemed to us to be far more impressed than such a straightforward job demanded. But the important thing about it was that people in the village knew that for practical help they could rely upon us.

We very soon had occasion to help over something more important. It was during the season of minimal viticultural activity that we were invited to lunch one Saturday by one of our nearer neighbours, the wasp-killer and his wife. Without their ever having said so, we knew very well that they benefited enormously from our presence in the village. They lived in a pleasant house all on its own and with a splendid view from the terrace looking across the vineyard we had acquired from Monsieur Julien, all the way to the distant coastal hills of the massif of La Clape. At any time this view could have been ruined for them by the erection of a house immediately in front of them. Provided we held the vineyard they were safe, and perhaps it was an unspoken feeling of gratitude that had led Monsieur Ruisseau to destroy Polly and her brood.

During the meal, Madame said was it not a disgrace that the chateau was sold to strangers.

'What!! The chateau? Sold??'

'And right under the nose of the mayor,' said Monsieur Ruisseau. 'Madame Bonnevoix warned him nearly three months ago, and what did he do? Nothing at all!'

'I have seen the letter she wrote to him,' Madame Ruisseau went on. 'It is a scandal.'

'Foreigners too,' said her husband. '*Anglais*. Er . . . excuse me, of course . . .'

I could smell immediately an outsize rat. The chateau of Montouliers had belonged partly to the family of Madame Clavel since I knew not when. Her aged mother had long lived in one half of it but was now reaching a condition that would make it imperative for her to be moved out and placed in the care of other members of the family. Some months earlier Madame Clavel herself had asked me if I would not like to see the chateau and give it a look over, as it was for sale. It was difficult to refuse without giving offence, so I agreed to pay a visit and see round the interior.

It was a wandering sort of a place, two steps up, one down, mind your head here and so on, and in not very good condition. Each room was, of course, entered through another, and a single water tap served the whole place, although, curiously enough, there was actually a loo. The windows looked out right over the village, facing south.

'It is only six hundred thousand francs,' Madame Clavel wheedled. And then in half a whisper, 'She already has an offer of five hundred thousand.'

'Tell your mother to accept it immediately,' I said. 'And thank-you for allowing me to see it.'

Time had passed, the old lady was looked after elsewhere in the village and the price had dropped to half the original demand, a figure at which it had now, apparently, proved possible to find a buyer. I did not need to be told who had arranged the deal; there was a foreign individual who prowled around the villages to arrange deals of this kind. Of course, he was doing the villagers a good turn by getting rid of their otherwise unsaleable houses; but the chateau – that was going too far.

There were two other sections of the chateau. Half already belonged to the village and was let out by the *Mairie* as lodgings for any odds and ends of unmarried mothers, or *vendangeurs*, or a family in need of accommodation. And a tiny corner at basement level was the house of Marie-Thérèse and her little papillon dog.

Marie Thérèse was ninety-two years old, very bent and with fingers clenched by arthritis. She was the most senior citizen and had not only an adorable nature but a very lovely face. She had never been married, although as a girl she must have been very beautiful. We often spoke to her when we met her outside the village, among the pines or on the plateau, her wide-winged bonnet over her head as she moved about to gather herbs, or the stems of wild asparagus, or the wild leeks which grew so easily among the vines, and, curiously enough, I found her one of the easiest to understand. She spoke a good French.

So what was now being sold was the whole edifice, minus the *Mairie* part and the humble dwelling of Marie-Thérèse. And once it was gone, there could be no getting it back again. I had always imagined the chateau to be *classé*, preserved for the nation, but evidently this was not the case. The news was saddening and the village was paying the penalty of being half asleep. There had been talk, emanating, in the first instance, from Les Cactus, about what an idea it might be to have a museum right there, in the chateau, of a village interior in the year 1907. The point about 1907 was that it was the year of the bloody vintners revolt and so of interest in itself.

Added to which, from being invited into village houses I was sure that utensils and other domestic ware of the period were still to be found on all sides in abundance and probably for the asking.

When, on the following morning, we drove into Montouliers on our way home from our usual market-plus-church expedition, we saw a group of people talking in the roadway by the *boulodrome*. Seeing our car, one of them, Madame Audirac, beckoned urgently to us to come at once. The party was an indignation meeting and was on its way to the mayor's house to give him what we used in Lancashire to call 'what for'. Perhaps Ingrid and I were not enormously enthusiastic, but we were concerned about what happened to the chateau so we obeyed the summons and went.

The mayor lived in a large house at the edge of the village. We filed into the hallway – his house was almost unique in having one – and through into the parlour, which was nearly as dark as night. Madame Fraisse swept some drying vegetables off the table, and we crowded around it, the mayor in the centre of one side and the rest of us spread round to complete the circle. There was an awkward hush, and the mayor placed his fingers together, took them apart again, and looked extremely dismal.

It was now time to start the 'what for', and two of the ladies set to in earnest. Had the mayor nothing to say? Was he not told months ago? Had he not thought of exercising his right to stop the sale of this, the jewel of the village? It was *incroyable*.

The voice of accusation rose higher and higher, and another lady chimed in. Though made of stern stuff, the mayor looked beaten down, trampled upon, desparing. It must have been his worst day since he took office more than forty years earlier.

When the ladies had run out of steam I ventured a question.

'Has the *acte* been passed? Has it actually been signed by both parties?'

The mayor looked up. Signed? He was not sure, but he thought so. Anyway, there was an agreement with the agent to sell it to the English purchasers.

'If the *acte* has really not yet been signed, it can be stopped, can it not?' I asked.

One of the men present said that was right. We should find out at once. Claudette should get on the telephone immediately to the *notaire* . . .

'It is Sunday.'

'Never mind. He probably lives in the same house as his office. Which *notaire* is it?'

It was the familiar lawyer of the Dutch widow, and of Monsieur Theysseire. Hearing that, I thought it extremely unlikely that the *acte* was already passed. He would be holding the money on deposit, I was sure.

The mayor cheered up a little, but his problems were not over yet. Supposing the sale could be held up, what then? The short answer, of course, was that Madame Clavel and her brothers and sisters – there were seven sharing the ownership, I understood – would certainly not agree to seeing the three hundred thousand francs which had been dangling in front of their noses suddenly whisked away.

'The village would have to buy it,' somebody said. And if the mayor looked as downcast as ever, the reason was plain. The price was not far off two thousand francs for every man, woman, child and dog in the place. The *Mairie* simply had not got that sort of money.

'But it is unthinkable . . .' one of our lady firebrands began. There seemed nothing to be gained by letting her fire another broadside at the mayor, so I intervened.

'It could be arranged,' I said confidently.

The mayor clutched at this straw like a drowning man. 'Arranged? How can it be arranged?'

'With a loan,' I said.

'But who would lend that sort of sum to the village?' It was Madame Meunier who asked the obvious question. She was not a native but came from Montchanin in Burgundy and she had a head full of sense.

'I don't know,' I said (That was true enough.) 'But I shall discover. Leave it with me, and I will see if we cannot get a cheap loan for five years.'

The meeting broke up, and we all went home for lunch. The mayor was so shaken that he never even remembered to offer round the muscat. But the first steps were taken, and it was agreed that Claudette was to get hold of the *notaire* at the earliest possible moment, and then, in case the English purchasers were adamant, to contact the departmental authorities, the member of parliament, the board of historic buildings and I know not what beside. As soon as she had news that there was a chance of stopping the sale I was to be informed, and as we were just on the point of returning to Jersey I said that when I got there I would start making enquiries anyway.

The *acte*, it transpired next morning, had not been signed. The *notaire* had the money on deposit and no doubt he would be able to have it there a few days longer. It was currently earning about eight pounds a day, which mounted up well as time flowed by. He agreed to stall the sale.

Next came the question of the English couple who thought they had bought the place. They obligingly agreed to drop it. I doubt if they knew how wise they were to do so, but I knew very well indeed. If they had stuck to the contract their troubles would only have begun. The drains were blocked? Nobody would be found to unblock them. The plumbing needed radically altering? Well, unfortunately there were serious difficulties about extending the piping. The roof leaks? A pity, but no builder has the time to see to that.

And so on. This was France, and if the couple from England (whose identity I asked should not be revealed to me) had eventually taken up residence in the chateau, their life would have been made one continual hell, and their dream of being the proud owners of a real chateau-fort in the Languedoc would have become a nightmare. Everyone in the village, however friendly under normal circumstances, would have been against them. I had no doubt at all that they were being saved from a very unpleasant fate.

After some days of negotiation and turmoil, Claudette phoned us in Jersey and said that all was clear. If they had access to the money the village would enter into a contract for the purchase. The following day I was able to telephone back that I could get an investment company to lend the money for five years. A loan agreement would be drawn up.

In the event, the agreement was drawn up in Stockholm. It was sent to the mayor for signature, and he was so overcome that he phoned me twice in Jersey, and I could sense that the excitement of being in contact with the international world of finance made his usually dry voice shake with emotion. Then he raised the question of whether the agent should not be paid for allowing the sale to lapse. But I said No. The loan I had arranged was for the chateau. The agent could jump off the pier. If anyone paid him, it could be the vendors of the chateau, but certainly not the village.

Curiously, the village had no bank account, or, at least, not one that could hold the money. I was asked to explain to the loan company that the cheque had to be made out to the Collector of Taxes in Puisserguier. This was not, of course, my business, but I strongly objected. It was in vain. The tax office took the money and very properly put it on deposit immediately.

Back in Montouliers once more, I enquired whether the taxman was intending to hand over the interest to the village. Claudette had not missed this point, but her information was that the interest would not be remitted. I said it was outrageous; here was the *Mairie* enjoying the chance of a loan, and the greedy-guts of a government office took their borrowed money and swallowed the profit. They should be given their own full share of 'what for'. The village ladies all agreed with me. It was a scandal, a swindle, it was trickery, it was *dégoûtant*. It was . . . France, a land where everyone in public office knows very well that somewhere, and in this case at the Puisserguier tax office, *il y a un homme plus grande que moi* whose authority may not be questioned.

The tax office was in luck. The agreement of, I think, seven separate and somewhat scattered members of the Clavel family had to be obtained before the sale could be made. I was round at the *Mairie* at least once a week to see if they had all agreed and the *acte* had been signed. Of course, it had not. Time went by, a week or two, a month, another month, and no sign of the *acte*. The *notaire* knew nothing about it, the taxman *non plus*. It was a scandal, a swindle, it was trickery, etc., etc., we all agreed.

One day I met Madame Meunier in the street. 'Ah, Monsieur Pilkington! Did you know the *acte* for the chateau was signed?'

'At last!' I jumped with delight.

'Yes. Several weeks ago. But nobody told us.'

The news that the village had actually bought the chateau spread quickly, and in no time at all a public meeting was called in the library of the *Mairie*. It had been decided by consensus that a society should be formed, full of ideas for restoring the chateau and developing it in some way, and generally presenting the village in a better light to the outside world. The last thing we wanted was to have the place become one more spot where English and German drop-outs sat around pretending to make the leather belts and purses which they got cheap from Hong Kong. We wanted ideas. One of them was to make two high-quality *gîtes* or holiday lodgings. There were cheap ones enough in Montouliers, occupied for two or three summer months, but there was nothing to compare, for instance, with the Chateau de Grézan near Lamalou. Ingrid and I had inspected the *gîte* in the gate-house at Grézan and found it comfortable and tasteful. It was well furnished and could accommodate five people, and it brought in seven and a half thousand francs a week. That was good money and they apparently had no difficulty at all in getting that amount from English or German families. Looked at in another way, it was not much over twenty pounds a head per night, and that was not ruinously expensive at all.

It was all very well to have ideas aired, but there had to be some sort of executive with authority. Hence the public meeting. Broad-beaming Monsieur Hortala, past-president of the wine co-operative, was at once shouted into the presidency by popular acclaim. The vice-president was similarly elected, and that was myself. I found it difficult to hear exactly what was going on because I was a bit hard of hearing, the language used by many seemed to be a sort of mixture of Catalan and Occitan, neither of which I knew, and the opening of the meeting with Monsieur Hortala's hammer on the table was a sign for general pandemonium. Nobody addressed the chairman. He beamed and so did I, whilst people in opposite corners of the room exchanged views on many intermingled subjects at the tops of their voices. We managed, however, to elect the other officers and establish an annual subscription which everyone would be encouraged to pay.

During a sudden lull the young manager of the co-operative vigorously raised a complaint. Why was Montouliers not named on the signpost at La Croisade, where two D-roads crossed? (La Croisade had nothing to do with the crusades – it simply meant The Crossroads.) There was some shouting about this and it was generally agreed that it was a disgrace. Madame Meunier, who was doggedly taking notes, said it would be drawn to the attention of the highways department of the Hérault. (It was. The name eventually appeared.)

It was now the turn of Monsieur Cathala jr, the *cantonnier*, the man in the official pill-box cap. He had a complaint too, about another disgraceful state of affairs. He dutifully swept the streets, shovelled up leaves and dog shit and had the village all neat and tidy, and what happened then? Every other day the advertisement men or girls from the supermarkets came charging through the village, stuffing into mail-boxes or under door-knockers their advertisements of the special bargains of the week at Montlaur, Leclerc, L'Univers, Cordial, or Super-U. With what result? If people were at home they merely took them out of the mail-boxes and threw them on the ground; if they were away from home the Tramontane did it for them. And there was he, a good, hard-working, honest *cantonnier* who kept the town tidy, and an hour or two later it looked like a rubbish-heap.

This kept people going for some time. The suggestions

included mine, that if the papers were all habitually either thrown away or blown away, we could perhaps mount a *poubelle* at the entrance to the village and request the supermarkets to have their rubbish dumped straight into the bin, unread. Monsieur Cathala, our stalwart *cantonnier*, need then only add the leaves and dog shit and we should all be happy. Especially the advertisement deliverers, who would be saved the chore of racing round the village with their bags of bumf and could go home early.

Not much was decided on that occasion, because it was more of a launching ceremony than anything else, but before long we had a meeting of the committee. All our faithful friends were there except for the wasp-slayer and his wife who never took part in any activities beyond bridge and scrabble. The meeting began at six, and this being the Languedoc most members had arrived in time for Monsieur Hortala to bang on the table with his hammer at half past.

We were eleven in the room, but there was more noise this time than ever. Madame Meunier smiled, pencil poised to make notes. Monsieur Hortala beamed in silence. I tried, but could make nothing out of what was going on, which was shouted altercations across the room. It sounded like anger, but obviously it was not.

At six-forty I asked the President in a whisper what we were supposed to be discussing tonight.

'Anything you like,' he said pleasantly. But I never got a word in.

At seven o'clock I said that I very much regretted having to leave, but we had visitors arriving at any moment. (This was true, and just in case anyone should not believe it, we displayed them to the village shop next morning.) I stood up. So did the rest of the gathering. It was the signal for the meeting to be considered over.

'I think we have discussed everything,' said Monsieur Hortala, putting on his coat.

We all said '*Allez, bonne soirée*' and I reached home two minutes ahead of our visitors.

A few days later, Madame Meunier called.

'I've brought you a photocopy of the nine items we decided the other night,' she said, handing over a neat sheet of decisions.

'Nine items? Decided?' I looked through the list. The decisions were properly recorded and seemed sensible enough.

'I don't remember any of these things,' I said. 'I can't recall any motion about anything at all, nor anyone addressing the chair, nor any vote taken either.'

Madame Meunier smiled pleasantly. 'Ah,' she said. 'Yes, but this is the Languedoc. You see, they don't work that way here.'

It was a month or two before we had another meeting, and the proceedings were opened by Madame Meunier cheerfully announcing that the mayor was otherwise occupied, and M. Hortala was unavoidably absent from the village. *Alors*, Monsieur Pilkington would be in the chair. This was not, the first time in my life that I had chaired a meeting, but it was certainly the first occasion when I would not be very clear what was going on. I knew however that the only subject for discussion was what to do when the party from Montpellier came to view the village.

The discussion was easy enough, for it merely consisted in deciding what we were going to show the visitors, and that was already a foregone conclusion. There would be the church, the chateau-fort, the cobbled calades, the Roman well, the prehistoric cave on our land, and then the opportunity of a free aperitif – and maybe the purchase of a bottle or two of wine – at the Cave Co-operative's tasting parlour, where an exhibition of photographs of the village in bygone years would also be mounted. The only matter for serious discussion was how many groups we were going to have. Should the visiting party be divided into four? No? Well, what about three, or maybe two?

A lot of conversation went on across the room about this vital matter, and in the end I decided to call a halt by putting it to the vote. Maybe they did not work that way in the Languedoc, but here was a real chance to show how a meeting would be conducted in other parts of the world. I banged on the table, and said we would vote on the matter. All those who, thought two parties would be best were to raise their hands.

They did. All the ladies voted for two parties to be shown round. Right. All those in favour of three parties?

The three men present raised their hands, and the chairman declared the matter decided. It would be two parties.

173

But there he was wrong. When the bus-load arrived in the village they immediately formed a single large herd to be led round from one place to another. But even if it was of no avail, the principle that one could actually vote on a matter and have the result recorded in the minutes by the competent Madame Meunier had at least been established. Maybe in the Languedoc they would indeed henceforward work in that way. But secretly I doubted it as much as the rest. Besides, I liked things to run the way they did.

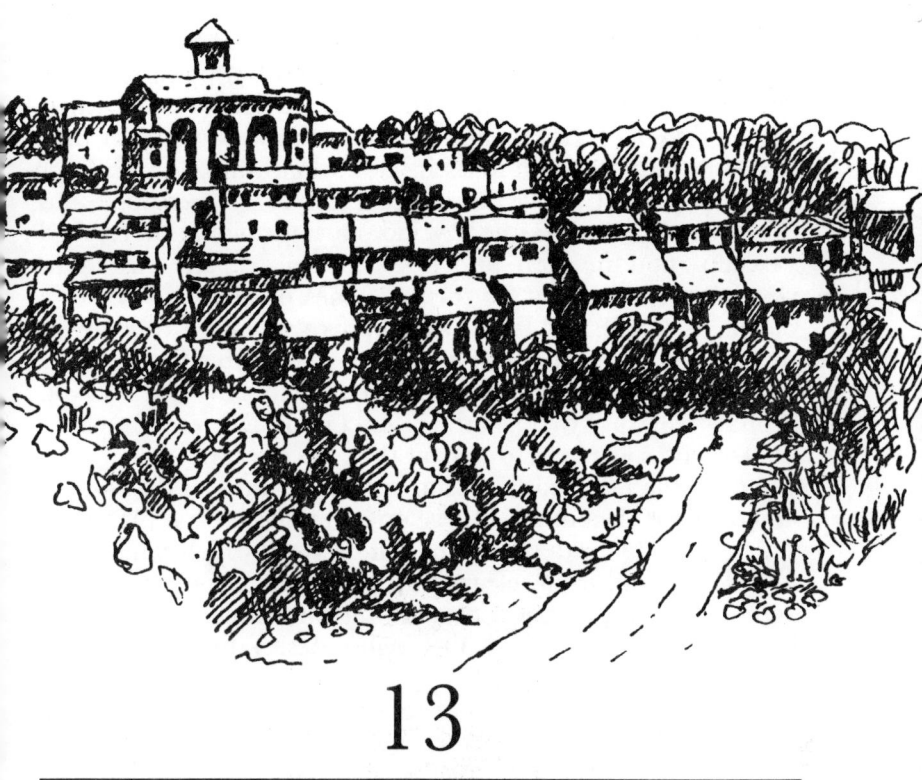

13

Not Without Problems

The year we moved from Soleil d'Oc we were too late for the *vendanges*. Not that we could have joined in very effectively, for the entire yield from our upper and only vineyard amounted to less than twenty kilos. The red we took home as grapes to eat – and rather pippy ones too – and the ten kilos of *terret* I squeezed through a dishcloth with the help of a rolling pin and actually obtained seven bottles of something that any person with defective tastebuds might have agreed was vin blanc. But we were not yet viticulturists. We were only taking the scrapings from a small and badly maintained patch of vines.

It had been a brilliant summer with hardly a shower of rain over the village, and while others were busy with the harvesting, we drove over to the high Corbières for a walk across the wild, arid plateau. Once again, we saw the formation of large birds flying at a great height and with slow but powerful beats of their wings. This time they were heading south, their summer sojourn in Holland or Alsace now over. Soon they would be gliding down to their winter haunt in Morocco.

On the plateau above the village the vines were stripped, and in another few weeks the myriad starlings would arrive and descend upon the spare bunches which pickers had missed, or which were abundant on the end vines of each row where a picking machine had been at work, because of the difficulty in turning the monster and having it in operation right from the end of the row. We called the spare bunches 'widows and orphans' because we liked the injunction in Deuteronomy that the Israelites were not to go over the rows a second time to pick what they had missed. It was to be free pickings for the widows and orphans. In our area these unfortunates were replaced by starlings in clouds that darkened the sky and which came down ahead of a cold front, cleared all the spare grapes over a few acres and then, at the command of some superstarling, rose into the air to wheel and turn before descending again a few hundred yards further on.

The signs of autumn were there in Montouliers also. The smart new sales parlour of the wine co-operative still had a few visitors, but not many. *Comportes*, large, two-handled and wash-tub-shaped oaken containers used for carrying the grapes from the vineyard to a waiting truck, lay inverted and newly rinsed over the gutter to drain. The dogs were still lying in the roadway or visiting their friends to go for a walk, the onion man still appeared on Wednesdays, driving swiftly through the village with his hand on the hooter and a boot filled with onions red and white. The fish van was stationed at the crossroads on Thursday mornings, the shoe-shop came once a month and so did the draper. These regular activities continued, but there was a feeling in the air that the year was running down. The slack season was at hand, the time for taking stock, and wondering what the future held for the wine-growers, and for the village, which was much the same thing.

Apart from the postmistress and the family that kept the village store, no trade other than that of wine-grower was to be found. The baker and chemist were in Argeliers, so were the two hairdressers, the fruiterer, an upholsterer, an ironmonger and a bar. The electrician and two garages and a restaurant were in Bize. Argeliers had four doctors, Bize four. The *curé* lived in Cruzy. The agricultural supply warehouse was in Argeliers. Montouliers produced wine, sold wine and drank wine. Full stop.

This dependence of the area on wine, and mainly on plonk at that, naturally tailed off toward the coast, where the seasonal tourist trade was the main industry. This summer influx of tourists made a slight impact upon Montouliers also, for many of the houses let rooms as *gîtes* from July to September. This brought in a little money to the households, but the customers tended to be those who could not afford the higher prices of the littoral although a few – such as our friends the Stormes from Ghent, and the Latinnes from Antwerp – came because they loved the village with its peace and absence of bustle, and with its excellent situation for excursions of all kinds. The Latinnes had taken their holidays in the rear of the mayor's house for the last forty years or more; the Stormes for a quarter of a century had taken simple accommodation in the main street. Both families were greatly liked in the village, and were completely at home in it. We always looked forward to their annual visits, because Professor Storme was in the cancer business just as Ingrid had been, and they had plenty of mutual acquaintances.

This dependence of the community on a single item of trade worried me. It also worried others, especially after the admission of Spain to the E.E.C. Sometimes the smouldering animosity born of fear of rivalry broke out in violence – though not in our own community which had, nevertheless, been involved in the great riots of 1907, as the exhibits of the village history showed. At that time it was not Spaniards who caused the trouble, but Algerians, and the wholesalers.

Before that time there was plenty of money in wine, as could still be seen in the faded magnificence of vintners' houses built toward the turn of the century and earlier. Huge gate-posts, fine balustrades and magnificent iron gates now sadly rusted, balconies, carved masonry, vast hallways and the remains of expensive hand-painted wallpapers, great fireplaces and even fountain-groves, all testified to the prosperity of the period when wine had sold at more than thirty francs a litre – and good solid gold-based francs at that. Within twenty years the price had dropped by four-fifths or more. The boom had led to overproduction, but there were two other factors – unrestricted import of Algerian wine, and adulteration by the large wine merchants, who found it cheaper to add water, and sugar from the subsidised sugar-beet.

The vintners of the Languedoc were faced with ruin, and it was from Argeliers that a leader emerged to head the revolt. Marcellin Albert, who is honoured in that village by a park and a statue, was so successful in rousing the men that an army of nearly three quarters of a million labourers and growers sacked the City Hall at Béziers and then marched upon Montpellier. A regiment was sent to check them, but being unwisely chosen, in that it consisted partly of the sons of vintners, it mutinied and joined the rebels. There was serious fighting in Narbonne before the government called a halt to the disorders by prohibiting sugaring, regulating imports, and, later, by a decree that every man among the millions of French soldiery was to have an issue of a quarter of a litre of wine daily. Calm was restored, but the golden days were never to return. And now one could see painted on walls and bridges such slogans as '*CEE = Ruine*'. or '*PS Traître*'. PS was the socialist party, which had failed to resist the entry of the Spaniards to the E.E.C.

Sometimes the ashes of resentment would be fanned by discontent, or failure of some kind. On one occasion three or four wine-men threatened the manager of a supermarket that if he did not take Spanish wine off the shelves they would do it for him. He took no notice, so the men returned and smashed all the bottles on the floor. They were soon joined by '*pompistes*' who destroyed the installations for cut-price petrol. Huge damage was caused, and eventually the men were rounded up and charged at the Court of First Instance. Where, naturally enough, the magistrate found that there was no case to answer . . .

Then one day I drove down to Narbonne to pick up a grand-daughter at the station. Turning in to the forecourt I was stopped by a soldier, armed to the teeth. No, I could not drive in to the car park, he said pleasantly. No.

I noticed that the whole station area was devoid of the usual collection of parked vehicles, and instead there were armoured cars. I thought it imprudent to stick an alien nose in, so I smiled and thanked the man, and parked nearby. As for the grand-daughter, she did not arrive. No trains were running.

I discovered from the paper next day that anti-Spanish wine-growers had gone on the rampage. They had managed to block the four lane motorway near the border by hijacking one or two articulated lorries. They had ordered Spanish lorry-drivers to stop and had turned their cargoes into the road and burned them. The main railway line from Paris to Spain was blocked outside Narbonne by piling-up and firing a heap of old motor-tyres. The railway signal-box at the crossing on the road to Cuxac had been burned out – not that the efficient SNCF had anything to do with the matter beyond the fact that the railway led to Spain. (There were, of course, no prosecutions).

I talked to Christian Bonnel about it. Was Spain's entry into the E.E.C. such a disaster?

'Not at all, mon cher Roger,' he said. 'The good grower has nothing to fear. He can hold his own against any Spanish wine that ever was pressed. This is the work of the incompetent, the feckless, those who cannot produce decent wine if they so much as try. They have reason, certainly, to fear the Spanish rubbish. But not the real growers. Certainly not.'

And yet the frustration smouldered, and could easily erupt. A year later the message *Tous à Narbonne le 28* began to appear throughout the area, the responsibility for spraying it in red upon any suitable surface being claimed by the Vintners' Action Committee, the political affiliations of which were not hard to guess, and which was not representative of the bulk of the vintners. And the growers had indeed a grievance, even if the best ones could overcome it, for the E.E.C. was reducing the amount of land under cultivation for wine, and at the same time the price of wine was falling.

The march upon Narbonne (not on foot, but by car and lorry) duly took place, but when the men arrived at the city they found themselves confronted by a strong military presence equipped with armoured cars. The reason for this had nothing to do with wine-growing, but was due to the fact that the *harkis*, descendants of those Algerians who had remained loyal to France in the Algerian war, and had left the country along with the French rather than stay there and have their throats cut, had been rioting in Narbonne, blocking the motorway and the main railway, piling stacks of old tyres and setting them alight wherever opportunity offered, in order to draw attention to their grievances. So the Action Committee supporters, full of

179

fire (and maybe of raw wine) found themselves frustrated because the rioting had already been let loose by others, and the chance of having any support for a demonstration of their own had gone. So, not to be thwarted, they turned away and made for Béziers, where they wrecked everything possible along the Allées Pierre-Paul Riquet, exactly where their predecessors had run amok and encountered the military eighty-four years earlier.

Getting rid of great quantities of not very high-grade wine at a reasonable price was necessarily a problem, and an idea which had been started in Burgundy some years earlier was now spreading to the Minervois – though in a much less polished and perhaps more honest fashion.

Montouliers itself began to produce '*primeur*' in November, and though that would never keep for more than a week or two, it was by no means undrinkable as a luncheon wine, provided one was prepared to accept that it was pure, unblended, unmatured, brand new, recently fermented rouge. Nobody pretended anything else. But in Burgundy it was different. Some brilliant person had hit upon the idea of a great advertising campaign to sell the raw newly pressed and fermented rouge not as immature hogwash but as something exceptional for which the world was waiting. Press, posters, television, every medium of advertising was employed to the full to work up the public abroad to a state of restless expectation, awaiting the day when it would be officially announced in Beaune that 'The Beaujolais nouveau is ready!'

It said a lot for the ingenuity of the advertising industry that it managed to work people up into a fever of expectation over a product that no Frenchman would wash his dog in. It was difficult to believe that people could be so taken in, but in Jersey men with Porsches and Jaguars and Mercedes would be standing by to drive to the harbour the moment the news came through, and would race day and night down France to buy a bottle of Beaujolais nouveau and get it back to the island ahead of others. Nor was this extraordinary phenomenon confined to Jersey. Men flew from Japan and the United States to be first home with the year's new product of something that was not worth a glass of mild-and-bitter. Of course, it was a wonderful thing for the villagers of the Beaujolais, who quickly organised a central bottling business to meet the demand, and so were

180

spared the months of patient tending and maturing of wine that was properly looked after. After which, with plenty of money and nothing to do, they could fly away to the Canaries or the Balearics for such a well-earned holiday as vintners previously had not dreamed of.

We had plenty of laughs down at the *caveau* of the co-op about the Anglais and their gullibility, but in the village Beaujolais nouveau was not stocked. Not even as a wood stain. In Bize Beaujolais nouveau could indeed be found, because there were enough foreigners resident in the vicinity. But the *primeur* of Montouliers was an infinitely better wine and nobody pretended that it was anything other than what it was, a drinkable, immature and rather sharp red wine which was adequate as a *vin de table* but had no further pretensions.

Probably the Beaujolais nouveau idea saved many a vintner in Burgundy. It led to huge sales with no nonsense about tasting and sampling, and a great saving of labour if the wine did not need to be stored and matured. The Minervois did not follow suit, and I always liked to think it was innate honesty rather than lack of imagination that led the growers to refrain from copying the *nouveau* idea, or for that matter the older-established Liebfraumilch trick of the Rhine.

All the same, the concentration of the village on a sole product was obviously dangerous. The E.E.C. might subsidise people to grub out their vineyards, but what then? Nothing else could be grown. Even with the vast pumping system of the Bas Rhône company, the soil dried too much. Where people had tried tomatoes, or sunflowers, or maize down in the plain, there was nothing to show for their efforts but an acre or two of dried, withered and useless plants and a big bill for the water hopefully and uselessly sprayed. Vines needed endless treatment, but at least they bore fruit, even in a drought. And survived for another year. That the system was not at all hopeless was shown by the number of fields grubbed out and replanted with new stocks, for throughout the first three years at least, these plants would be eating fertiliser, sprays and tractor fuel without giving anything in return except hard work.

That wine-growing was a feasible activity provided one worked hard was obvious enough. Most of the men in Montouliers had a presentable car quite apart from the vineyard van or truck. The families were well-dressed; the Argeliers hair-salons had no lack of lady customers. Huge televisions, larger than anything we had ever owned (or would have tolerated) graced every living-room. The young had noisy motor-bikes, and some of the toys thrown away on the village dump were by no means cheap. Evidently there was money around, cash enough for a life which had no enormous expenses.

Vintners rarely, if ever, took a holiday, for the simple reason that during the traditional spring and summer vacation periods they were hard at work. In fact, the only time that some of our village friends had ever been away from home was when the *curé* hired a bus and organised the trip to see the Pope in Rome. Some spoke Catalan or Spanish, for the frontier was only an hour's drive distant, but not one of the residents spoke English, or had been to England – and that was why the presence of M. Pilkington-Fixit was so useful in translating the sales literature of the *caveau*, and even recording three tapes, in English and German and Swedish, which told visitors much of the history of the place and introduced them also to the wines produced there.

It came as a surprise to me to find that none of our leading citizens appeared to have ever heard of the great new inclined plane or water-slope at Béziers, one of the great and best-known engineering wonders of modern France and only twenty minutes distant. Few had been to the Corbières hills. The horizon was much, much closer – in fact, just beyond the end of the row of vines. People were content in their village, chatting in the *épicerie* (ladies) or on the seats under the mulberries next to it (men) or on the steps of the 'Roman' well (older and sometimes amorous teenagers) or under the arch that led to the calades or steep cobbled alleys (first-year motorbikers).

One day when the ladies came up to borrow some more watercolours, Madame Audirac noticed a painting of a chapel down in the bottom of a gorge. Where, she asked, was that?

'Saint Jean le Trou,' I said. And as that name evidently meant nothing to any of them I added, 'It's real name is St. Jean Dieuvale'. Hole, or Vale of God, it mattered not. None had ever so much as heard of the chapel of St. Jean, which was only fifteen minutes distant.

In a way, I could not blame them. I only discovered it myself when Madame Cabanes, who was on some sort of departmental committee concerned with restoration in the Hérault, happened to mention that work was being done on the roof of St. Jean Dieuvale. I asked her where it was.

'It is useless to explain to you,' she said with a brusque gesture. 'You would never find it. It is beyond St. Jean de Minervois, but unless you knew where it was it would be a waste of time trying to visit it. No, you could never discover it.'

This blank refusal to give me the location because, I imagined, of my assumed foreign stupidity (as shown by the shape of our re-styled chimney-pot, which I guessed she had not forgotten) was enough to make me determined to track the chapel down. In fact, it took me three days. On the first, driving up all the most inviting *chemins* which twisted over the *garrigue* to the north and east and west of the muscat vineyards of St. Jean de Minervois, Ingrid and I had a piece of luck. One little road ran to a dead end in a tiny hamlet, Gimios, and there on a wall was painted a faded sign of the kind used by cartographers to signify a church or chapel. An arrow pointed along a rather brambly *chemin* which led to more fields of muscat.

We followed all the vineyard tracks without success, but next day I returned and followed a rabbit track (or perhaps the path of a theoretical *sanglier*) amid the honeysuckle and scrub oak. Through a gap in the bushes I could see that the land fell away vertically and going to the edge I saw, several hundred feet below, the chapel at the foot of a dry gorge. It took us another day to discover the track leading down to the bottom of the *trou*, so Madame Cabanes was probably right at least in so far as she thought it useless to explain to me how to find the place.

As the ladies had never even heard of the place so close at hand, we invited Madame Audirac and the Meuniers to come and see it next day, and perhaps it was during this expedition that I realised that we ourselves were inquisitive by nature, and perhaps others might be reasonably content with a calm if busy life in their own immediate surroundings and felt no need to look any further.

In the village the facilities for education were good. There was an infant class in the village, and after that it was a matter of the school bus to Quarante and later to Capestang or Béziers. The young were all around the village at weekends and on Wednesdays, the no-school days. But I could not see them settling down to a life of up-before-the-lark and working until dusk in the fields. Their own horizons extended further as a result of schooling and of television, and it was clear that there was plenty of intelligence around. Young people left the village and did well in the world outside, coming home in their vacations to visit the family, and the place they still loved. Talking one day to a grower to whom the whole world more than a few miles distant was completely unknown, I discovered that he had bought a book of mine in English (which he could not read) to send to his daughter, who was head of a department in the head office of a French bank dealing with London.

The fact that the younger generation was not very likely to become resident in the village was only one of the causes of houses becoming empty. Another was the television. Not only in the ceaseless advertising but perhaps especially in the American soap operas which were ground out of six channels throughout most of the day and half the night, the housewife could see others living in *plainpied* (single-level) houses with kitchens, and dishwashers and every mod con the studio could haul out of the repository, and the sight of these accessories of civilised living would sooner or later make a family wonder whether the time had not come to build a new, airy, single-level house on the edge of the village. All across the Minervois and neighbouring areas the trend was the same. The cramped village centre was becoming empty and abandoned, and a new ring of standard off-the-peg villas surrounded the former community. Life was slowly becoming modernised, at least as far as the ideal home was concerned.

This was also borne out by the telephone calls. We had only been a month or two at Les Cactus when we received the first of many.

Ingrid answered. Somebody wanted to speak to me, but she could not catch the name.

I took the receiver myself. '*J'écoute.*'

'Ah, bonjour Monsieur Pilkington. *Comment allez-vous?*'

I said I was fine, thank you. Who was calling?

'Arlette!'

Arlette. Who on earth was Arlette, I wondered, mumbling some non-committal platitude.

'I have tried several times to get you on the phone,' the

sweetly wheedling French female voice went on. 'And now, here we are at last!'

'Yes.'

'It is so nice to talk to you.'

'Yes?' Could somebody have tried a dial-a-date or a naughty-naughty line and dialled the wrong number?

'I hope I am not disarranging you, Monsieur Pilkington.'

'Oh, no . . . not at all.'

'*Bon*. I had it marked in my diary; *coup de téléphone à Monsieur Pilkington*.' A polite giggle, then. 'Ah! Well, this is me, Arlette. And I just want to ask you something.'

Advice? Confession? Was it a *sondage*, a poll of opinion about some item of French foreign policy? '*Eh bien*,' I said, and waited.

After the first few months I knew exactly what was coming from Arlette, Marie-Françoise, Delphine or Simone. Had I got a kitchen?

Yes, I had a kitchen.

'*Excusez!*'

'*C'est rien.*'

'*Au revoir*,' said the voice, so honeyed that I could almost smell the Chanel No. 5 down the wire.

It was usually a kitchen, but sometimes a bathroom that they wanted to sell us. The firms went right down the pages of the telephone directory, but they never spoke with the lady of the house. Only with the men. Perhaps the male was thought to be more easily wheedled, and very likely that was correct.

These phone calls made us realise that plumbing in the village houses was probably rather limited, and as we came to see more and more homes from the inside we could see that it was true. The largest house in the main street was for sale, and though the building was substantial enough to have entrances on three separate levels in different alleys, the whole edifice was served by one single cold tap in the kitchen. As time went on we became familiar with many of the village houses, and although some now boasted a '*salle d'eau*' with a basin, shower and loo, we never once saw a bath. Even the *salle d'eau* was obviously a recent addition.

A family who moved out into a new easy-to-run two-bedroom house needed to sell their old one. But there were no buyers. Village people wanted to move out, not in, and more professional families like doctors wanted plumbing, and proper electrics. Very often the wiring in the older houses was exceedingly amateur, carried out with bell wire stapled round the door frames. Anybody buying a house inside any of the villages would find it necessary to run up large bills for the services they would need to install. And the houses themselves had another particular disadvantage; every room was approached through others, so if there was a toilet, or a water-tap, one might have to tramp through two or three bedrooms if caught short in the night. This was France . . . but in this case France was best allowed to become *passée*, I thought.

Étienne's house had been up for sale for four years, and there were no takers. It stood in the middle of the village, close to the *épicerie* and the spot where the market vans stopped. There was nothing wrong with it except that it was built in the style which had the staircase leading from one room to the next and so on right through the house. Below the standard of the *maison de maître*, that was the way things had always been, but the very nearly twenty-first century *Homo sapiens* did not want it that way any longer, and unfortunately the arrangement was almost impossible to change.

By now, however, most houses were at least connected to the sewer. One could see the man-holes in the road, and toilets would flush properly whereas kitchen- and bath-water (shower water in reality) still ran out of a hole in the wall into the gutter. One always knew when somebody was washing, or taking a shower, or cleaning up in the sink, because the run of water at the edge of the street or down the centre of an alleyway was there for all to see.

I asked Étienne about the sewer. 'Can you explain the system,' I said. 'I can see that most of the houses are on the sewer, but I don't see any sewage plant here. Not even at Argeliers.'

'*Non-non-non.* There is none,' he said, looking very wise.

'But Étienne, what happens to the sewage?'

'Ah, Monsieur Pilkington. That just stays in the main drain, and then once in a while they let down a big flush, a wave from the *chateau d'eau*, and it's *fini*.' He made an explosive gesture.

I considered. 'I can see that. But where is it flushed to?'

'It goes into the village stream,' Étienne replied. That was the gulley which ran below our vineyard, passed under a bridge by M. Julien's house, and wended its way through the vineyards into the distance, presumably to end in the Canal du Midi, east of Argeliers.

'But Étienne, that stream has been dry as a bone for two years past at the very least,' I said.

'*Bien sur.* That's why you have this bad odour when the wind is the *vent de la mer,* from the south-east.'

I understood. *Bien sur.* And it probably saved a lot of unnecessary expense to arrange the system in that simple way.

'*Impeccable,*' I said. And that was that.

There were other reasons beside lack of plumbing that made it difficult to sell a house, and chief among these was the family. Sometimes a house might belong to a whole band of brothers and sisters, either because it had been left in equal shares in a will, or because intestacy had worked that way in fulfilment of the French inheritance laws, or because by spreading the ownership one could mitigate the effect of death duties, as only the owner of a fraction of the total would die at any one time. This was ingenious enough, but it assumed a basis of trust and something at least approaching understanding in the family. It had proved satisfactory when Madame Clavel's family had sold the chateau to the village, presumably because all the sisters and brothers wanted their share of the takings. But that was not always the case.

Monsieur and Madame Barroubio lived in a house near the top of the village, with a terrace and a fine view right down to the cathedral of distant Narbonne. It was a tall house which was three storeys high, two fronting on to the lower road and one backing on to a narrow street above. It was the top floor in which they lived, and it was a pleasant house but a bit too small. However, the lower storeys which opened to the road below were ruined, and had been so for years past. Cracks had now begun to appear in the upper portion, and obviously the house would one day collapse if nothing were done to restore the ruined lower sections, which lay wide open to wind and rain, crumble and rot.

Monsieur Barroubio wanted to repair the whole building but there was nothing doing. His brothers had a finger in the pie of ownership, and I gathered that one of them disliked the second Madame Barroubio, a person we ourselves very much liked.

Frustrated, the Barroubios decided to clear out in time, build a new villa outside, and sell the older premises to somebody who would reconstruct the whole building. But again, nothing doing. The family would not agree to a sale either. So the Barroubios had to move to their new house and leave the old one empty, unoccupied and not even up for sale. Pigheadedness of this kind was often thought more important than making the most out of a property and sharing the proceeds.

But assuming that all the family members owning a house were willing to sell and had agreed, temporarily, to bury a whole assortment of family hatchets, that was not the same as having a ready customer. In fact, there were only three possible kinds of purchasers. First there were Parisians and others from the north who might buy an old house and convert it into a holiday home for themselves and their families. Then there were the foreigners who might pick up a house for the same purpose. There was also the danger from speculators and roaming agents who came to villages in the Minervois and tried to acquire property cheap with the intention of selling it again at a good profit later. Finally there were individuals who might be pleasant enough, but who were quite unable to understand the way of life in a village such as Montouliers. Back home their day began at nine and probably ended at midnight, and they did not fit into an environment where life was so utterly different, and where neighbours, tired after a long day in the vineyard, were not likely to appreciate the habits of suburban night-life, which might take the form of late night barbecues and parties far into the small hours, occasions inevitably attended by sleep-destroying noise.

For village life ceased after supper. By nine at night the vintner families would be in bed, ready for a five o'clock rise as dawn broke and it was time to take the bread, dip it in the coffee, and start getting together the equipment for the work of the day ahead. We often took a walk through the village after dinner, and except in the *gîte* season it was unlikely that we would see so much as a chink of light or catch sight of any living creature other than a cat – the dogs were early bedders too. One could hear crickets, and maybe the Scops owl down among our olive trees near the brook, but otherwise there was not a sound under the clear and starry sky of fading dusk. No

Village life ceased after supper. By nine at night
the vintner families would be in bed

traffic, not a man-made sound. That was one of the many beauties of Montouliers.

A couple from Paris whom we very much liked, and who greatly cared for the village, had bought as many as six houses in a state of ruin, and were restoring them. They were suspected by some to be taking advantage of the village to make money by reconditioning and selling, but this was quite untrue. As some other villagers realised very well when we discussed it, this couple was doing the village a good turn which few could afford. Every one of the old houses they acquired as ruins was saved from collapse or destruction. They were all being properly and sensibly restored in good and simple taste, and were put in the absolutely reliable ownership of other members of the same family. Such an action undoubtedly saved them from being acquired by just the kind of people nobody wanted to see coming over the horizon – rock stars, Hong Kongers, developers, boutique owners and the second- or third-rate artists and potters who so quickly congregate together and destroy the whole atmosphere of a community with which they have nothing in common.

We often talked with village people about this difficult matter. There was no actual right of veto vested in the mayor – and that was probably as fortunate for the village as it must have been a relief to him – and yet the community had no funds to buy and restore, and in any event it had its hands more than full with the acquisition of the chateau-fort, bravely bought on borrowed money. The only hope was that houses becoming vacant be acquired in time by our Parisian friends, by one other public-spirited individual who had bought property in one of the calades, and, of course, by the Pilkington-Fixits.

We did not intend to have this mantle of restoration dropped upon us, but when we examined the matter over a suitable draught of Cuvée de Mayol, one of the better wines from the wine co-op of which we were so happy to be members, we felt certain we knew individuals enough among friends and relations who would take over little houses of great charm (and little plumbing) and use them for vacations, or for gradual retirement, until perhaps they would actually live there. The important thing was to act, and act quickly to save the houses whenever opportunity arose; to restore and, if necessary, hold them until they could be transferred safely to sensible ownership.

190

People in the village were co-operative. They loved the place, and a glance round the memorials in the cemetery was enough to convince us that most of the families had been in Montouliers for a generation or two at least. But if they were moving out into more modern dwellings it was hardly realistic to expect them to refuse any buyer who came along. They needed the money for their new house, and it could not be demanded of them that they should turn away an agent who said he could sell the old one, or a purchaser who, from the community point of view, might be thought not quite what was wanted.

There was no communal society to take care of the sale of houses. The Association for the Preservation of Montouliers had no funds for that sort of activity, and it fell to private individuals to do what they could. That was how it came about that we began with our one incomparable home of Les Cactus, for which we could every day give humble and very hearty thanks, and two years later had also the *Écurie*, a charming little house built in 1632 and one which was to be in use throughout the year by the increasing number of family and friends who came to stay and certainly appreciated as much as we did that we did not wait upon the order of their day, nor they on ours. Next it was to be the *Boulangerie*, which had not been used for some years because the village could not eat baguettes enough to keep a baker in reasonable affluence, but which contained the finest oven front one could ever hope to see.

And after that? It might be the end, or it might not. We, and others, had continually to be on the alert to see that the village belonged to the village, and that if parts of it were sold and restored, it was only to people upon whom we all could rely; to individuals who would appreciate the place not as an investment, but as something lovable for what it was. People who would, in fact, love Montouliers as Montouliers, and its villagers for being the gentle, kind, sunny, hard-working, smiling, generous people they were.

14

Viticulteurs Récoltants

The final day of our first year at Les Cactus ended with the Pyrenees shining pinkish in the sun of late afternoon, and the plateau above Montouliers spanned by a splendid rainbow against a sky of fading blue. It was not cold, and the morning of the New Year was so warm that a red squirrel muttering, 'To hell with hibernation' scampered up a poplar close to the house. It was time for me to look in the shaving mirror and wonder if what I saw there could possibly ever become a *vigneron.*

The answer was 'Yes'. With nineteen degrees in the shade at midday, the time had also come to discard the pullover, roll up the sleeves and get busy with the pruning. Only some eight or nine hundred vines to clip. *Only* . . .? It seemed a mighty task, but I was soon to discover that this quantity of *souches* was nothing compared with what others tackled. Broad, jovial M. Babeau who bumped away to his vineyards every day as soon as the sun was up had one hundred times as many. Cheerfully, he clipped away single-handed at his four-score thousand vines as though his life depended on it. Which of course, it did.

For myself, the pruning was a task of absorbing interest, but it was not a case of living on the proceeds of the vineyard. The work was good exercise, but it was more than that. For the first time in my life I really felt bound up in the cycle of seed-time and harvest that the assurance of the rainbow brought home to me each time it came to span the ridge with its spectral colours. And with a sun as bright and strong as a Scandinavian midsummer it was no hardship to move slowly along the geometrical rows, snipping.

Christian Bonnel came over again from Aigne to show me how to tackle the job. After the leaves have fallen, a vine is crowned with a wide entanglement of branches a couple of feet or more in length, and as these mix with those of their neighbours and may even grab hold of them with tendrils, to approach a bush closely to clip it is not particularly easy. It is for this reason that most wine-growers like to give the bushes a first 'haircut' a foot or so above the main trunk, and then prune more accurately later. At first sight this seemed to me both a waste of time and energy, but having tried to prune both trimmed and untrimmed vines, I was soon convinced that the labour-saving method of a single pruning did not, in fact, save labour. The double haircut system was less frustrating than trying to disentangle oneself from a spider's web of very tough and twisty branches.

However, it was a year or two before that method was fashionable, so we began in a more straightforward and laborious way. The first action was to stand back and regard a vine-stock like an artist critically viewing the subject of his portrait. The main stem would have split into several lesser ones, which might be four or five or more in number. Any one of these, if 'joli', could perhaps carry two reduced stalks for the following year. Stems with not much to show for themselves could be cut right out, if need be, with a saw – for vinewood is extremely hard – and those halfway between good and poor might be allowed one shoot. Ideally, a healthy vine would be permitted seven sprouts for the following year, less fully grown plants six, or five, or four, according to their shape.

Having stood back, clippers in hand, and having carefully observed the field of operation, one was then to attack the vine with care and affection until the requisite number of joli sprouts were left, each reduced to a length of two inches or less, the clip being made above a bud and preferably one which directed itself upward and outward.

I liked pruning, and after the vines had been shorn of the unwanted branches, they looked to me like a collection of little black men or women dancing energetically and with their arms raised in ecstasy at the thought of what they were going to achieve in the spring after their winter sleep. As for the branches chopped off, these had to be collected to get them out of the way, and Étienne and I would range them in neat heaps between the rows. Madame Real – by now I was becoming weary of hearing how she arranged things – would tie them into bundles to save them, he said. I knew this very well, as I had already spent an afternoon clearing from the garage great quantities of vine branches decayed and dusty, but it was soon established that we were not in business to pick up sticks or collect rubbish and store it, but would burn the clippings just as other wine-growers did.

Our vineyards were both on sloping ground, so we man-handled the clippings to the edge and lit useful bonfires. (Provided the Tramontane was not blowing of course). But the slope meant that it was not practical to construct a portable bonfire such as many of the growers used in their vineyards down in the plain. These ingenious devices were not difficult to make. An oil-drum cut in half lengthwise, a few holes knocked in the metal to admit the draught, the chassis of an old perambulator spotted by watchful eyes to be sitting forlorn on a village dump, a handle long enough to tow the contraption between the rows when pruning, and that was that. During January, the plain below the village always had the columns of bluish smoke drifting slowly in the nearly still air to show where these ingenious fires on wheels were plodding through the vineyards at a rate of perhaps one-twentieth of a mile per hour. These pleasant plumes of smoke rising from the brown or whitish or reddish field to fade away against a sky of the intense blue of the Midi were so quietly beautiful that I always longed to paint the scene. But I never did. The absolute geometric rows of little dancing men were a natural and intriguing feature of the countryside, but when put on paper they looked – there are no other words for it – damned stupid.

Early in the spring it was time to put on the fertiliser, which meant driving down to Argeliers and, after throwing pebbles for the amiable Alsatian watchdog to chase and fetch with insatiable activity, loading a few sacks of nitrate. Other and much larger growers were doing the same, carrying away their haul in tractor-trailers or decrepit Renault vans which once had belonged to public utilities. In their case, the nitrate would be spread by a machine with a revolving disc, towed behind the tractor, but in our vineyards it was distributed by Étienne.

His system was, in theory, both simple and effective. After the rare event of enough rain to soften the otherwise brick-hard clay he would walk along the rows making a good hole above each vine with a single hefty blow of his *pioche* or mattock. Into this he dumped a plastic cupful of fertiliser granules and pushed the earth back over them. Then when the rain came later it would run through the loosened earth, dissolve the fertiliser and distribute it through the surrounding soil. So the whole vineyard had a grid of points from which the nitrate would be spread uniformly over the whole. *Voilà!* Nothing could be simpler – *bien sur*! Next year the holes would move round through ninety degrees, so that after four years one would be back where one had started. Each year it was just a case of a hole, a cup of the right stuff, and the rain did the rest.

Only it didn't. Because sometimes it never arrived, or such rain as came during the summer was no more than a suspicion of dampness when the Tramontane gave way for a day or two to the *vent de la mer*. One autumn when I was trying to remove with a spade some suckers of elm roots which had a way of coursing through the vineyard, I happened to dig into the pockets where the fertiliser had been inserted. It was still there, a cupful by each vine, but I doubt if any of it had passed into the plant during the six months when it could have been wanted.

We soon discovered that the wine-grower was to be engaged in a ceaseless round of treatments against oidium, mildew, rabbits, and a host of weeds which seemed to flourish (as did the vines) in the absence of water. Étienne took command of this warfare and he had his own equipment. He would arrive one morning in his van, from which he unloaded at the side of the lane a number of twenty litre *bidons* of water, into which he stirred the soup of the day, a Bordeaux mixture or some highly specific poison produced by the chemical industry. He then ladled the fluid into a tank which he slung on his back and walked several miles during the morning as he passed up and down the rows working the pump handle with one hand and directing the clouds of spray with the other. I admired his persistence. It was a messy job, and the back-tank was heavy, yet he whistled as cheerfully as the nightingales while he tramped along the slope, dressed in an ancient army jacket that had the colour and the smell of an arsenal of chemical warfare.

This spraying was undertaken several times each summer, and seemed effective. Étienne was very observant, and at the first sign of red mites, or mildew, or oidium or any other unwanted organism appearing on the leaves or the burgeoning bunches he would mount an attack, which usually seemed

195

successful. By the end of our first season I began to have a suspicion as to why the *vin de pays* had such a strong tang of *je ne sais quoi*. For months the fungicides had been landing on the grapes and drying *in situ*, and the real wonder to me was that nobody seemed any the worse for ingesting these chemicals in their glass of wine.

Our upper vineyard was amenable to a cultivator provided the ground was first softened by a downpour of rain – a rare and unpredictable event. Showers tended to be non-existent, or perhaps once a year so violent that branches were broken off trees, our lawn was littered with debris from the pines, the gravel was washed out of our driveway and the vineyards on the plateau above had their soil piled up in the roadway. In fact, the rain, when it came, was usually exciting.

Often when driving through the Minervois and the neighbouring areas, we would see a warning beside the road to the effect that the *chaussée* was *submersible par forte pluie*. As these roads were usually raised several feet above the surrounding land, such an event was obviously impossible. The very idea that the road could be under water was ridiculous, and when near Capestang we passed posts along the verge on which the depth of water was marked up to a metre or more we thought the local highways department was either ridiculously pessimistic, or hysterical, or both. It could not possibly happen. Not conceivably.

One day we went for a trip on the Canal du Midi with some friends from the States who had a most attractive iron barge, *Mon Rêve*, built about the turn of the century and converted inside into the most comfortable mobile *maison-de-vacances* that I have ever seen. The Downeys loved our area and came over each year for a season of voyaging, and, as so often before, we were with them for a day, starting, on this occasion, at Sallèles-d'Aude and ending about a dozen locks further west at Homps, where we had left our little Renault so that we could drive Dixon back to Sallèles to fetch the little car which he usually carried on deck.

It had rained in the morning before we took off. It was only a shower, but it was heavy enough to fell a large pin parasol across the canal at Sallèles. By the time the engineers had winched the tree to one side, the day was cloudless and the vineyards basked in the warmth of the July sunshine. On our way back toward Sallèles that evening, passing along a road we had driven that same morning, we came to a notice, 'Route barrée!' Road repairs, I thought. All the same, we can probably manage to get by.

But it was not road repairs. Ahead round the bend we found the road completely submerged. Water was pouring across it for a distance of a hundred yards or more, fence posts, vines and stakes bobbing on the current that bore them away. At either side of this unexpected river a number of cars were waiting, together with one rather foolish individual who had tried to rush the flood at high speed, with the result that the water had surged over the motor, and who was trying to push his car and girl friend out of the torrent. I took off my shoes and socks (I was, of course, wearing shorts through all the summer weather) and, having looked inside the bonnet to see how high or low the first risk of electric short-circuit was situated, I walked slowly in front of the car while Dixon drove very cautiously behind me, able to see from my legs how deep the muddy torrent ran. The road was flooded just to the bottom of my knees, and those knees, we had decided, were the limit of safety. So, like the Israelites, we passed over.

This road was not even marked as submersible, so the depth on the highways so described was probably greater. But I could now see how such floods happened. Somewhere there was a modest stream, possibly even dry, which passed under the road in a culvert. A sudden deluge, a swiftly swollen stream bearing on its bosom plenty of rubbish to block the hole, and the road would act as a dam. The water rose inexorably; the roadway was submersible.

Shortly after this there was a heavy downpour over the city of Nimes. Such a place consists, of course, in the main, of impermeable surfaces – roofs, pavements, roadways and streets – but Nimes happens also to be built on a slope with the oldest part of the town at the bottom. So the water poured off the roofs and concrete and tarmac, and the street drains could not cope with such a flow. The torrent rose, and hundreds of cars parked along the roads were swept away like corks. This extraordinary mass of detritus surged onward to jam the alleys of the old town and fill them to the height of the first floor windows with crumpled Renaults and Citroens, BMWs and whatever else had been left at the parking meters.

197

One night we were driving home late from a concert, and near Capestang the road (a submersible one) was obstructed by branches smashed from the plane trees by the sheer violence of the rain, and by the banks of orange clay washed out of the vineyards. Yet five miles ahead at Montouliers there had, as usual, not been a drop of water. On another occasion we were anxiously phoned by friends and relatives in Sweden who had seen in *Svenska Dagbladet* a photograph of people canoeing across a road junction in Narbonne, with the caption that 90 centimetres of rain had fallen in four minutes. Well, it had certainly rained, but not as much as an extra '0' inserted by the type-setter suggested.

But we can leave the rain and return to the springtime tasks of seeing that everything possible was done to ensure a good grape harvest. Our lower vineyard being on too much of a slope for ploughing, the flourishing weeds and grass had to be removed in some other way. Étienne said we needed to use Rernderp. He repeated it several times and asked if I would get some.

I said yes, I would, and when one of the village vintners emerged from his customary and lengthy lunch I asked him if he used a herbicide.

'*Bien sur*, Rernderp.' That was what he would recommend.

So I drove to Argeliers, threw pebbles for the Alsatian while awaiting my turn, and then boldly asked for a can of Rernderp. Nobody seemed surprised at this demand, and the storekeeper said Rernderp was excellent, although there was one common weed of the vineyards which was resistant to it. He then went off to the store and returned with a two-gallon *bidon*. It was a product of the Monsanto Corporation, and its name was Round-Up. The price nearly caused me to faint – I think it was just over one thousand francs – but on reading the instructions I discovered with relief that the proportions set out for the diluted spray meant that we had enough for at least five years of spraying.

In fact, the Round-Up rounded up all the weeds extremely well, except for the one resistant species. I had to wait for a very still morning to avoid the slightest drift of spray on to the vines, and then march down the rows, spraying the ground as I went. I tried to avoid the dark blue muscari which were beginning to bloom so nobly, and I passed over one or two patches of the wild leeks which we liked for salads. But a light mist of herbicide settled on the rest, and a few days later they yellowed, wilted, and collapsed.

In March the shoots were sprouting, and by April the first tiny bunches of grape flowers were being fertilised and soon were setting as minature trusses an inch or so long. The branches lengthened by several feet, shaking hands with those of their neighbours. The leaves were a beautiful green under the intense blue of the sky. When a violent blow of the Tramontane descended upon the vines, the branches which reached up high above the stocks would sway and twist, and to prevent their breaking we would run down the rows to strip off some of their leaves. The wind, said Étienne, must be allowed to pass through the bush and not smash it.

Spring in the Minervois was a time of great beauty. So was any other season, but in spring we had the wonder of the hillsides bright with pink cystus and the pale blue of rosemary, and the perfumery aroma of Spanish broom drifting on the breeze. On the stony plateau crossed by our red-marked track, thousands of tiny golden narcissi stared up at us as we walked, and in the wet meadow along the Cesse near Bize a taller, multiflora one, paper-white with an orange trumpet swayed in the wind that blew down the valley. Wild Judas trees, the envy of any botanical garden in Britain, made broad patches of veinous blood along the edge of the pinewoods of Le Pech, and tall bluish-purple irises were everywhere. One almost wondered why people bothered to have a little plot of garden with such a glorious show on every hand. Inevitably, one recalled the Song of Songs, for the winter was past even if the rain was not over and gone (because it had never come). The voice of the turtle was not there to be heard, but the Scops owl took its place, and the fig tree was beginning to put forth its figs. However, it was not the foxes, the little foxes, which spoiled the vineyards; it was the rabbits, or would have been had we not taken precautions.

Rabbits were not a danger to established vines, but they had a liking for the leaves of new ones where we pulled out an over-aged stock which had ceased to be reasonably productive and replaced it with a new one, or better still, by grafting a short piece of branch from a neighbour into the existing root. We could keep the rabbits off by placing bright blue nylon netting round the small plants, and I liked the appearance that this scatter of blue stockings gave to our slope. It was also a sign that we were not inclined to let things go, and our first spring we replaced sixty stocks with new ones. About forty of these were carignan, one of the basics of the plonk industry, but the rest were a scatter of dessert grapes – muscat, chasselas and Italia.

How vines manage to extract from an arid soil or stony desert enough water to transpire and flourish and build great quantities of grapes containing so much fluid has always been a mystery to me. But they do. All the same, after three months of scorching sun it was clear that ours would not refuse a drink if such were on offer, especially at the time when the grapes were really beginning to swell. Montouliers was, of course, on the Bas Rhône irrigation supply, and it was this theoretically endless supply of untreated and very cheap water that enabled us even to have a lawn of sorts, provided it could have a good sprinkling every day. The only trouble was that the big vintners in the plain had their giant sprays going, and Montouliers lay a little higher and was right at the end of the pipe-line, which meant that the pressure was less and fell almost to zero at the height of the watering season. The final piece of piping led to Les Cactus and two houses outside the village, and in high summer we had to have a watering agreement, each of us confining ourselves to two hours between dawn and the main spraying time as morning advanced. I chose eight to ten, and I think we all abided honestly by the treaty, though what happened after dark was another matter.

We also had two wells, one in the upper vineyard and one under our terrace. Miraculously both seemed always to have water only ten or fifteen feet below ground level, so I acquired an electric pump which was powerful enough to cover all of our vines in turn. At the same time it was important not to cause a plague of mildew by spraying when the air was hot and dry, and there was also the risk of over-watering so that the vines took up enough to make the grapes actually burst. In all this we relied upon the judgment of Étienne, who had three little vineyards of his own and a lifetime of experience. And I could see that he was determined that our entry into viticulture should be a success.

One morning at the end of July Étienne summoned me to the upper vineyard in a state of excitement.

'*Regardez*, Monsieur Pilkington. *Couleur!*' He pointed to a truss which showed the beginnings of a purple hue in some of the grapes.

Colour appearing in the grapes. That, I knew, meant six weeks to *vendanges*. It seemed to be an invariable rule.

A month later discussion was running high in the village as to the exact date when the *vendanges* would be declared open. Already the wine co-operative was buzzing with activity as vats were hosed out. Rivers of pinkish residue flowed down the gutters, lengths of flexible piping lay in the road, the sound of hammering on steel pipes and valves echoed from the *cave*, and men gathered by the tanks to sample just once more the wine of the previous year as it was pumped this way and that to leave room for what was coming. Articulated lorries dumped mountains of new bottles, some with the special moulded arms of the Minervois. Giant road-tankers came and went, the notice 'Alimentation – Lebensmittel' making it quite clear that they would not explode and so might be permitted to traverse built-up areas. As the opening day drew nearer, friends in the village would warn us never to leave the house unlocked, not even for a moment. The *vendangeurs* would be coming, and – well, one never could tell.

The *vendangeurs* were of several kinds. They did not tend to be gypsies, as the work was too hard. The main flood came from Spain. Already notices in Spanish were appearing in the Narbonne and Carcassonne railway stations in preparation for the score or more of special trains which arrived each day, packed with families of Spanish pickers. Wine-growers at Montouliers tended to have their regulars who were booked in advance and came year after year, but vintners from other villages would drive their trucks to the station yard to fill them with eager workers as they came off the trains. Besides these there were rather feckless families from the industrial north who would arrive in creaking vans and old trailer-caravans and park under the trees near the canal to try their luck as pickers, or perhaps as house-breakers; and there were the students who hitch-hiked to the sunny south for the delight of the experience and the prospect of a week or two of work which was not too highly or too meanly paid. In 1990 the pay was likely to amount to about twenty-five pounds or more for the day, with a pound or two extra for the lads who had the really tough job of *porteurs*, carrying on the back a sizeable sort of cornucopia into which the pickers emptied their buckets, then walking to the edge of the field, climbing a short wooden ladder and bending forward over the edge of a hopper-trailer so that the load fell down over their heads and through their hair, to be taken away eventually for pressing. The smell must have been with them for weeks.

The trouble with students was that they knew the *vendanges* would be a wonderful experience, but they had no idea how hard the work would be. And hard physical work was something to which many of them did not take very well. They got sore backs, headaches, stiff joints and other complaints at which point they were likely to decamp and leave their employers stranded without labour.

Christian Bonnel, himself a man of dynamic energy, was also very public-spirited where young people were concerned, and one of those uncommon Frenchmen who looked forward to an era of greater European co-operation. So he was open to take students, and at his vineyard near Mailhac he would house twenty in a happy community. Ginette cooked for them. He built a swimming-pool. There was a lawn to lie on and enjoy the sun after a hard day's work. There were all the facilities to make vendanging at the Domaine de la Lecugne as happy an experience as one could have, he told us. But then . . .

'Then?'

'Well, I took twenty young people. They came from Germany, Denmark, Britain, anywhere. The first day they worked hard. The second, they worked in the morning. The third, they were just in the pool, or lying in the sun. They did not want to work. Oh yes, they liked to be here, *pas de problème*; but work? I had to hire Spaniards to do their work for them. Well, I thought maybe I had had bad luck. I would try it again next year. And I did – with the same result. One day of work, another of a few hours, then – *fini*! It was fini for me, too. I never had *vendangeurs* again. I bought a Californian picking machine. It cost as much as a small house but it paid. My son drove the harvester and a single Spaniard walked behind it with secateurs and a bucket to take any bunches that had been missed. Instead of employing twenty, we had only that one man. Ridiculous. Stupid. Sad. But . . .' he made a gesture of resignation, 'what could I expect? If they did not work at their colleges, why would I expect them to work here?'

Christian Bonnel was, in fact, the first in the area to have a picking machine, but within five years they were to be seen all across the Languedoc. Monsieur Babeau in Montouliers had one which he used for his own vines, but he carried the cost of it by hiring it out by the day to other growers, though only with himself as driver. These machines worked best on large areas where the ground was fairly level, but they had one disadvantage which probably had not been foreseen by those who owned them, such as our friends the Couquets who had the Domaine de La Boulandière at the edge of the Corbières. There was a sudden heavy shower, the ground softened, and the huge machine sank into the clay under its own weight. There it sat, immovable, an expensive white elephant, and there was no other labour to be had. The Spaniards, no longer wanted, had gone back to Spain, and the Couquets lost much of their crop, which could not be picked.

Another unforeseen disadvantage was observed two years later in Montouliers. There was a light drizzle one morning, and the pickers hung about in the village until after lunch, to give the grapes a chance to dry a little. But some growers were on the go with harvesters and found to their dismay that when they had delivered their loads to the co-operative they ended up by having to pay a fine for the load being below the minimum density of sugar content. Human pickers picked the trusses, and a little water made very little difference. But the machines harvested by beating the bushes, and the rain-water on the very large area of leaves was knocked off to join the rest in the hoppers, so that the wine-to-be was very much watered down. And for that there was a penalty.

With the *vendanges* approaching, we had to book our own pickers. We reckoned that if we had two, they and I could manage the job in a few days, with occasional help from Ingrid. We would only take youngsters whom we personally knew, and we did not even pay their fares, let alone any wages. They came from Sweden, with the exception of Kenneth Storme, who came from Ghent and knew Montouliers well, his family having spent their summer holidays in the village throughout his life.

Our system was to have a reasonably early breakfast and be in the vineyard by eight. We gathered grapes till midday, had our lunch, and then went off for some exciting excursion or other, such as walking the ledges in the cliff face above Minerve or bathing in the rock pools of the Gorge de l'Heric, or swimming in the Mediterranean. The whole enterprise was a great success, and while on the job our *vendangeurs* worked hard and loved it.

We each had secateurs, and cut the bunches into the broad buckets that are designed for the purpose. These were carried to the lane when full, and emptied into dustbins and *comportes*, which we then loaded into the Volvo and the Renault, to the tune of three hundred kilos or more of red grapes, the aramon and carignan only being picked.

It was a drive of only two minutes to the co-op, where we might wait a few minutes while the hopper-wagons of those ahead of us were tipped into the weighing hoppers, but then our turn came. Our number was eighty-seven. As soon as one of the hoppers was empty, a stainless steel slide closed the bottom opening and we could back up with our load and tip the bins and *comportes* in. The needle on a big scale showed the weight, which was automatically printed on a ticket. The slide was pulled back, the grapes began to disappear through the crushing rollers, and down in the basement one of Étienne's sons would take a drop of our juice in a simple device which consisted of a small empty prism and a scale. When filled with juice, the prism would bend the light rays, and holding the gadget up to the light one could read the density of the fluid directly.

'*Onze huit,*' the voice would come up.

'*Onze huit,*' the hopper manager would repeat. The figure was added to the slip, which was pushed into a paper clip which travelled across to us by means of a pulley running on a long thin rod. We congratulated ourselves, and set off to start collecting enough for another load. Eleven-point-eight was good, but some loads were even better.

By the fourth day we had finished the red grapes, and the pile of tickets showed that we had carried down some two and a half tons of rouge, at a very satisfactory average density. Next day we would start on the white.

Harvesting the white was a very pleasant occupation, because we carried out the entire process from picking, through pressing, to maturing, bottling, and eventually drinking, our own wine. We had thirty or more bushes of terret in the upper vineyard, a good grape to eat and one with a very distinctive taste, with perhaps just a touch of almond to it. The colour was not as white as Riesling or Edelzwicker, but had a faint blush of pink to it. These bushes yielded about one hundred and twenty kilos of grapes, and within a couple of hours we had picked them clean. We then drove the load down to the co-operative. As members, we could use the small press which stood in the open beside the tall storage tanks, and we had booked it for the morning.

Apart from the attention of the dozens of wasps, which had heard a rumour that the Pilks were pressing on that particular morning, we had the press to ourselves while the delivery of rouge went on ceaselessly across the road. The wasps seemed less interested in the rouge, perhaps because it was not so sugary. We had first to assemble the press, then we put the first half hundredweight or so of terret within the circular cage of stout wooden laths, placed the round board on top, added the pieces of railway girder to distribute the pressure evenly, and began to crank the press down. At first it seemed that nothing was happening, but soon the cloudy juice tinged with pink would begin to seep out, trickle down, and come pouring round to the lip where it was delivered into a bucket.

We bailed continually, filling one thirty-litre cask after another, and by lunchtime we were on our way home with the full barrels. These merely had to be left alone to finish the job, with the bungs only loosely inserted.

Three days later, listening at the bung hole, one could hear the fizz of fermentation. We left for Jersey, secure in the knowledge that the wine would produce itself, for we had already asked Christian how to set about vinification. What had we to do?

'*Rien.*'

'*Rien?*'

'*Absolument rien.*' The wine would take care of itself.

Returning for Christmas, we found the wine quiet, fermented and maturing. A quick sample sip was reassuring.

Come February we could siphon out the fluid into cubitainers and run it through a coffee filter into bottles, one hundred and twenty of them. Soak the corks, force them in, and paste on the labels which we had run off in fours on the photocopier at the *Mairie*. They showed a pleasant little sketch of Les Cactus,

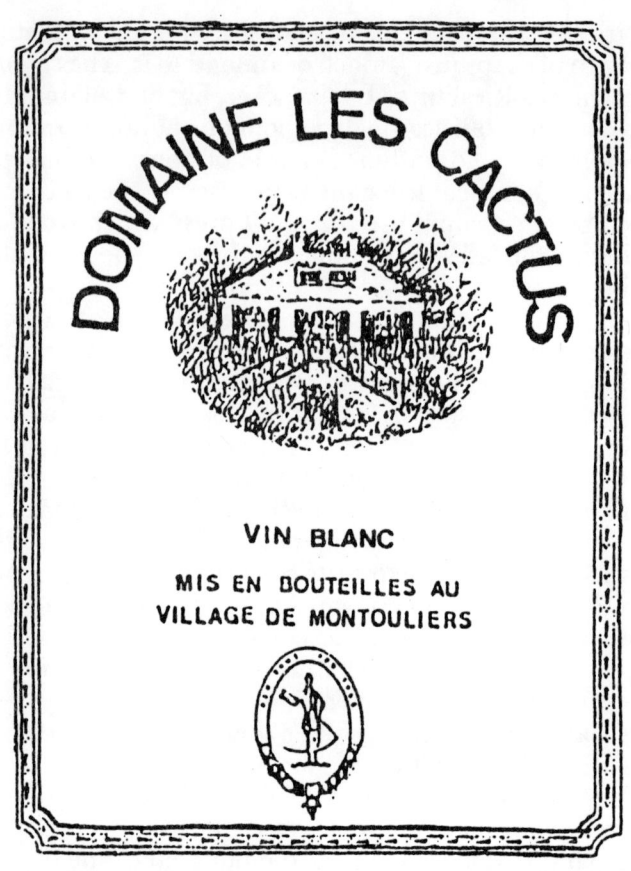

VIN BLANC

MIS EN BOUTEILLES AU
VILLAGE DE MONTOULIERS

done by Agneta Stålhand, who also did the charming sketches for this book.

'*Domaine Les Cactus*,' the label red. '*Mis en bouteille au village de Montouliers.*' And on the reverse of the bottle a neatly printed label bore the family arms and the legend '*Maintenant comme ci . . . maintenant comme ça.*' (This was a rough translation of the family motto 'Now thus, now thus,' and did not imply that the wine might be off.) '*Roger et Ingrid Pilkington, viticulteurs récoltants à Montouliers.*'

We had arrived. So had the wine, which was excellent.